TEACHING FOR TENURE AND BEYOND

TEACHING
FOR TENURE
AND BEYOND

Strategies for Maximizing
Your Student Ratings

FRANKLIN H. SILVERMAN

BERGIN & GARVEY
Westport, Connecticut • London

Library of Congress Cataloging-in-Publication Data

Silverman, Franklin H., 1933–
    Teaching for tenure and beyond : strategies for maximizing your student ratings /
Franklin H. Silverman.
        p.   cm.
    Includes bibliographical references and index.
    ISBN 0–89789–757–9 (alk. paper)
    1. College teachers—Tenure—United States.   2. College teaching—United States—
Evaluation.   3. Student evaluation of teachers—United States.   I. Title.
LB2335.7.S55   2001
378.1'21—dc21   2001025315

British Library Cataloguing in Publication Data is available.

Library of Congress Catalog Card Number: 2001025315
ISBN: 0–89789–757–9

First published in 2001

Bergin & Garvey, 88 Post Road West, Westport, CT 06881
An imprint of Greenwood Publishing Group, Inc.
www.greenwood.com

Printed in the United States of America

The paper used in this book complies with the
Permanent Paper Standard issued by the National
Information Standards Organization (Z39.48–1984).

10 9 8 7 6 5 4 3 2 1

Contents

Preface

It is difficult to win a game without having a good knowledge of its rules and strategies. Getting promoted from assistant professor to associate professor and being tenured can be viewed as a game that has both rules and strategies. This book is intended to provide college and university faculty who have a tenure-track position and graduate students who will be seeking such a position with some of the information they need to play the game successfully—that is, be promoted and tenured, survive post-tenure reviews, and receive merit salary increases. Specifically, it focuses on the rules and strategies of its teaching component, in a manner that is both practical and candid.

By viewing college teaching as a game, I'm not intending to demean it. I've been a college teacher for more than 30 years and am a recipient of my university's teaching award. I'm viewing college teaching in this way because I've found when mentoring junior faculty that doing so makes the dynamics of the process more understandable to them.

Also, to play a game successfully, you must understand its "unwritten" rules and strategies as well as its written ones. Unfortunately, there is a risk of appearing cynical when you describe a game's "unwritten" ones. My goal is for this book to be as helpful as I can make it. Consequently, I didn't avoid describing "unwritten" rules and strategies to protect myself from appearing cynical.

While departments differ somewhat in their requirements for promotion and tenure, most have ones pertaining to the following three areas: teaching, scholarly publishing, and collegiality (service). While the requirements for the latter—collegiality—may not be specified, a perceived lack of it is a frequent reason for someone to be denied promotion or tenure. Promotion and tenure committees, however, tend to avoid using collegiality as a reason for denying promotion and tenure for legal reasons. It is illegal to discriminate against someone on the job simply because you don't like him or her. Instead, committees will try to document some weakness in teaching or research. Teaching is an area they're likely to choose if a candidate's student ratings and other indices of teaching quality are not exceptional. Consequently, to maximize your likelihood of winning at the tenure game, you should both behave in a manner that is unlikely to cause your colleagues to question your collegiality and strive for a teaching record that clearly exceeds their minimal expectations.

Several of my graduate students (functioning as research assistants) and I interviewed a number of undergraduate and graduate students and experienced college teachers about some of the topics and issues that are discussed in this book. Much of the information presented in it was abstracted from these interviews.

It isn't possible to give credit to the many sources from which the ideas in this book have been drawn. This book is the result of more than 30 years of involvement with college teaching and the tenure process as well as hundreds of hours of conversations with persons in academia about both, particularly faculty at Marquette University and members of the Text and Academic Authors Association. Thus, I cannot credit this or that idea to a specific person, but I can say "thank you" to all whose ideas I have borrowed. Some special thanks are due to Erin Gartland, Amy Marcum, Melanie Martin, Ann-Marie Naber, Amanda Thompson, and Amy VanderHouten for their painstaking and probing interviewing of students about factors that affect the ratings they give teaching.

1

Teach Acceptably or Perish!

College teaching is unique as a profession. Job security and advancement (i.e., promotion and tenure) are largely determined by the excellence of performance of tasks other than the one the person was hired to do (i.e., teach). Such tasks include publishing, securing extramural funding (grant writing), and being willing to function as a team member, including doing a fair share of committee work and advising (collegiality).

While teaching well, by itself, is unlikely to yield job security and advancement for an assistant professor, a failure to teach well (e.g., receiving low teacher ratings from students) can reduce the likelihood of achieving both, unless he or she by the end of the probationary period has developed a strong national reputation as a scholar (through publications) and/or has generated a great deal of extramural grant funding. At the very least, it is highly likely to keep him or her from being awarded promotion and tenure before the "up or out" year. During my 30-plus years in academia, there was rarely a case in my college of someone who didn't have excellent teacher ratings being awarded promotion and tenure before the end of their probationary period. The few exceptions were persons who had generated a great deal of extramural funding and/or had exceptional publication records.

While teaching well, by itself, is unlikely to yield job security and advancement, not doing so is likely to make it more difficult to achieve both. Therefore, unless you're willing to risk your future on becoming a publishing and/or extramural funding superstar, you'd be wise to invest in becoming at least an adequate teacher, because doing so reduces the likelihood of your perishing (i.e., being terminated by the end of your probationary period). Furthermore, unless it's a "turn-on" for you to be hated by students, teaching well can make your job more enjoyable!

Persons preparing to enter college teaching usually receive little or no formal instruction on how to do it well. This lack of formal instruction appears to be based on several assumptions. One is that future college teachers can learn to teach adequately by emulating how their professors did it while they were students and/or by trial and error during their probationary period. It is certainly true that most of the current generation of tenured professors learned to teach in these ways.

A second assumption is that content, not method, is what is important in college teaching. Consequently, a person who is knowledgeable about his or her field and is smart enough to have gotten a Ph.D. should be able to figure out how to teach it to students.

A third assumption is that teaching well is not particularly important in academia, because excellent teachers who have marginal publication and/ or extramural funding records are less likely to be promoted and tenured than marginal teachers who have excellent publication and/or extramural funding records. Consequently, it would be prudent for junior faculty to devote most of their time and energy to achieving excellence in scholarship and grant writing rather than in teaching.

A fourth possible assumption is that a professor is likely to get more "payoffs" from being successful as a scholar than from teaching well. Possible payoffs include merit salary increases, a national reputation, job security, and personal gratification.

It certainly wouldn't be sensible for persons seeking tenure to invest considerable time and energy in teaching during their probationary period if these assumptions are valid. The situation, of course, would be different if they aren't valid or if their validity is uncertain.

If you aren't convinced that these assumptions are invalid or that their validity is uncertain, you're likely to invest very little in teaching. People are unwilling to invest when they don't—realistically or unrealistically— anticipate a substantial return from their investment. One way that you may be able to gauge your awareness of the possible benefits and losses from investing in teaching (and, consequently, your motivation to do so) is to answer the following hypothetical questions: "If you became an excellent teacher, in what ways (if any) would your life be affected? Specifically, in what ways (if any) would you be likely to benefit from achieving this goal? And in what specific ways (if any) would you be likely to be hurt (i.e., lose) by investing in achieving it?"

We will focus in this chapter on these four assumptions as well as on some of the potential benefits and losses from investing in teaching. We will also consider the role of teaching in promotion and tenure decisions and how teaching well can facilitate acquiring an adequate publication record for tenure. Hopefully, for both you and your students, the potential benefits from investing in teaching will appear to outweigh the potential losses from doing so.

ASSUMPTIONS ABOUT THE NEED FOR TENURE-TRACK COLLEGE FACULTY TO LEARN TO TEACH WELL

We will consider the validity here of each of the four assumptions referred to previously.

You Can Learn to Teach Well by Emulating How Your Professors Taught While You Were a Student and/or by Trial and Error During Your Probationary Period

These, of course, are the ways that most (perhaps all) of your professors learned how to teach, as well as how most of the current batch of college faculty probably learned to do so. For some, these methods both have been and are adequate for learning to teach well enough to be tenured. For others, however, they are probably inadequate, by themselves, to establish an adequate teaching record for this purpose.

There are a number of reasons why these methods could be inadequate for learning to teach well enough to be tenured, including the following:

- The faculty by whom you were taught were not particularly good teachers.
- The teaching strategies to which you were exposed were not particularly effective.
- Teaching strategies that were utilized by professors you want to emulate are not compatible with your personality and/or status.
- The current generation of students differs from yours in ways that are likely to affect both their expectations and learning preferences.
- The students you will be teaching differ from you with regard to motivation and learning ability.

Each of these is dealt with here.

The Faculty by Whom You Were Taught Were Not Particularly Good Teachers

Being a teacher is similar to being a parent in at least one way. As a parent, you are likely to discipline your children the way that you were disciplined. As a teacher, you are likely to teach the way that you were taught. It is quite likely that most (perhaps all) of your professors taught you the way that they had been taught and that their professors taught them the way that they had been taught. In fact, it is conceivable that the teaching methods to which you were exposed were developed prior to the invention of motion pictures, telephones, radio, television, and computers, or even the discovery of electricity! This, of course, doesn't necessarily make them inappropriate.

A teacher may not be particularly effective for reasons other than using outdated methods. He or she may, for example, lack the ability to create and/or reinforce an enthusiasm for learning in students. Strategies for dealing with these and other factors that can adversely affect teacher ratings (and, consequently, the likelihood of being tenured) are provided elsewhere in the book.

When selecting a professor to emulate (i.e., to be your role model), you would be unwise to choose one who isn't nationally recognized as a scholar. Investing in teaching at the expense of scholarship can also reduce the likelihood of your being tenured.

The Teaching Strategies to Which You Were Exposed Were Not Particularly Effective

If the teaching strategies to which you were exposed while an undergraduate and graduate student were at least close to the state-of-the-art with regard to effectiveness, this concern wouldn't be relevant. Otherwise, of course, it would be. Perhaps answering the following questions will help you to gauge how effective they were:

- While you were a student, did you usually feel that class time was well spent?
- While you were a student, did you usually feel that the assignments you were given were worthwhile (i.e., facilitated meeting course goals)?
- How well did your instructors motivate you to learn, particularly in required courses?
- How competent did your instructors make you feel with regard to course content?
- Did your instructors inspire you to achieve academic and/or professional goals that you didn't think you had the ability to achieve?

Your answers are likely to indicate that the teaching strategies your professors used were not as effective as they could have been. They, of course, may not be sufficiently lacking in effectiveness to reduce the likelihood of your being tenured if you decide to emulate them.

Teaching Strategies That Were Utilized by Professors You Want to Emulate Are Not Compatible with Your Personality and/or Status

The effectiveness of a particular teaching strategy may be determined, in part, by the personality and/or status of the person using it. Having a good sense of humor, for example, can increase the likelihood that undergraduate students will attend to lectures about material that isn't of particular interest to them. And being a full professor with a national reputation can make it easier to motivate graduate students to want to do well in your classes than if you are a beginning assistant professor.

Being successful as a teacher does not require you to have a particular type of personality. However, it does require you to teach in a manner that is compatible with your personality. Consequently, if you attempt to emulate a professor whose personality is very different from yours, the result may not be what you want it to be.

If a professor you choose to emulate is one who is highly respected and has a strong national reputation in your field, be aware of the fact that his or her success as a teacher may be related, at least in part, to his or her reputation. Students, for example, who might be willing to risk coming to one of your classes unprepared might be unwilling to risk doing so to the class of a professor who has this type of reputation. Before attempting to emulate such a professor, try to gauge how much his or her success as a teacher is related to his or her status, rather than his or her teaching strategies.

The Current Generation of Students Differs from Yours in Ways That Are Likely to Affect Both Their Expectations and Learning Preferences

The current generation of students is the first to have had the possibility of utilizing computers for learning since early childhood. For some of their computer-assisted learning, incidentally, they utilized video-game devices, which are "dedicated" computers. Furthermore, the current generation of students is the first to be both comfortable and competent using the Internet. Consequently, emulating how your professors taught your generation, which was probably less computer literate, may fail to meet the needs and expectations of students now as well as it did yours. This is particularly likely to be true if lecturing was the main teaching method utilized by the professors you are emulating.

The Students You Will Be Teaching Differ from You with Regard to Motivation and Learning Ability

A common complaint of beginning college teachers is that their students, particularly their undergraduate ones, don't seem to be as motivated and able to learn as they expected them to be. While their students may actually be at the lower end of the motivation and learning-ability continua, the perceived lack is likely, at least in part, to be one of perception. That is, they are likely to be comparing the motivation and learning ability of their undergraduate students to that of themselves and their fellow graduate students. Graduate students (particularly doctoral ones), as a group, tend to be smarter and more motivated than undergraduates. Consequently, teaching undergraduate students the way that your professors taught you in graduate school may not be particularly effective.

Content, Not Method, Is What Is Important in College Teaching

Content certainly is important in college teaching. A person who doesn't understand, at least intuitively, the concepts and principles he or she is attempting to teach is highly unlikely to be able to teach them in a way that students can understand, regardless of the adequacy of his or her teaching methods. To teach something to someone, you have to understand it!

That said, it is also true that without communication there is no learning. Telling students something doesn't necessarily communicate it to them. There are a number of variables that can influence the success of teacher-student communication, including the following:

- The amount of attention that the students are paying to the teacher.
- The means by which the teacher presents material.
- The manner in which the teacher presents material.
- The motivation of the students to understand the material.
- The students' certainties regarding their ability to understand particular material or do particular tasks.
- The motivation of the teacher to have most of the students understand the material or learn to do a task.

These variables, which tend to affect each other, are discussed below.

The Amount of Attention That the Students Are Paying to the Teacher

For a message to stand a chance of being transmitted successfully, the person to whom the message is being sent must pay attention to the person transmitting it. That is, the person to whom a message is being sent must set his or her filters to abstract the message, that is, to have the message be the "figure" and everything else the "background." If students are having their own thoughts during class or are attending to something in the classroom other than the teacher, the teacher won't be the "figure" and, consequently, the students are unlikely to learn very much of what the teacher is attempting to teach.

How teachers present information can affect their ability to hold their students' attention—that is, to be the figure rather than the background. A teacher who presents information in an organized manner is more likely to hold a student's attention than one that doesn't, as is a teacher who uses examples that are meaningful to the student and who interjects humor into his or her lectures. Consequently, focusing almost exclusively on content is unlikely to yield an adequate teaching record for promotion and tenure, regardless of whether the record consists of students' evaluations or measures of the amount they learn.

The Means by Which the Teacher Presents Material

How material is presented influences how well it is learned. There are a number of ways material can be presented including lecturing, textbooks, websites, video- and audiotapes, classroom discussions, the Socratic Method, assignments, simulations, CD-ROM tutorials, and hands-on experience (practicums and labs). Some are more effective than others for helping students learn particular kinds of material. There is, incidentally, a huge literature on the relative effectiveness of these strategies.

The Manner in Which the Teacher Presents Material

As I have indicated elsewhere, how a teacher presents material—particularly while lecturing—influences the amount of attention that students will pay to him or her and how much of the material they will absorb. The better (the more logically) that he or she organizes the material, for example, the more likely it is to be meaningful to them and, consequently, to be absorbed. A number of strategies are described elsewhere in the book for presenting material so as to maximize the likelihood of it being meaningful to students and absorbed by them.

The Motivation of the Students to Understand the Material

A necessary condition for students to learn is a desire to *know more* and/or *be more*. It isn't safe to assume that students are aware of why they should want to *know more* about what is being taught—that is, how the information can enhance their life now or in the future. This is particularly likely be the case for required courses outside of their major. Nor is it safe to assume that students are aware of how the information being taught can facilitate their *being more* than they would be otherwise. The ability of a teacher to convince students that an understanding of the material he or she is presenting is relevant to them is likely to influence (perhaps determine) their motivation to learn it and, consequently, the amount of it that they are likely to learn. This topic is dealt with further elsewhere in the book.

The Students' Certainties Regarding Their Ability to Understand Particular Material or Do Particular Tasks

Peoples' certainties (assumptions) regarding their ability (or lack of it) to understand or do things affect their ability to understand or do them. They become self-fulfilling prophesies. If students believe that they lack the ability to understand particular material (e.g., statistical analysis) or to learn to do particular tasks (e.g., certain ones involving computers), they are likely to invest very little in trying to understand or learning to do them and, consequently, their certainties are likely to be reinforced. A teacher who encourages (i.e., challenges) students to question and test certainties that are impeding their ability to understand course-related concepts and principles or to master course-related tasks is more likely to be regarded by students (as well as chairpersons, deans, vice presidents for academic affairs, etc.) as teaching well than one who doesn't.

The Motivation of the Teacher to Have Most of the Students Understand the Material or Learn to Do a Task

A professor who gives brilliant lectures may communicate concepts and principles well to only the brightest students in a class. Similarly, he or she may only be successful in teaching the brightest students to do course-related tasks. Such a professor may attribute the failure to communicate well to the majority of students to their being mediocre and/or not trying hard enough to understand, rather than to his or her teaching methods being inadequate. To teach well, you must communicate well to the students you have, rather than to the ones you wish you had!

Teaching Well Is Not Particularly Important in Academia

A case can certainly be made for an assistant professor's publication record and success in grant writing being given greater weight than his or her teaching record in promotion and tenure decisions in some (perhaps even in the majority of) departments. One assistant professor, for example, reported being told by a mentor only half jokingly that "If you're in consideration for a teaching award, then you're doing something wrong." Additional evidence of the value that the faculty and chair of some departments place on undergraduate teaching is their low level of concern about and monitoring of the activities of teaching assistants and their tendency to assign introductory courses to persons merely because they have ceased being productive as scholars (Kimball, 1988).

There is, however, another side to this issue. Few department chairpersons would choose to support an assistant professor for promotion and tenure about whose poor teaching students complain constantly. Dealing with student complaints is an activity that few department chairpersons enjoy. Consequently, the thought of having to continue doing this, perhaps until he or she retires, can be sufficient to motivate a chairperson to want to eliminate the source of the irritation—the assistant professor. His or her answer to the question that all chairpersons (as well as members of promotion and tenure committees) are likely to ask themselves when deciding whether to support someone for promotion and tenure—Can we do better?—is likely to be yes, unless the person has *and is likely to continue to* generate large amounts of extramural funding for the department.

There is at least one other reason why poor teaching may provide an

opportunity to not support an assistant professor's tenure bid in departments that care little about teaching. It is a more legally and politically
acceptable reason for not doing so than is a lack of collegiality. One of the
more frequent reasons why an assistant professor isn't supported for tenure
by his or her department is a lack of collegiality, or willingness to function
as a team player. The person may, for example, be unwilling to do his or
her fair share of committee work and student advising. Or the person may
function in a way that creates or reinforces divisions within the department
that impede its ability to function well as a team when it is important for
it to do so. A less than adequate teaching record, in such a case, would
tend to be regarded as a more legally defensible reason for denying tenure
than a lack of collegiality.

A Professor Is Likely to Get More "Payoffs" from Being Successful as a Scholar than from Teaching Well

A case can certainly be made for this assumption being true. An assistant
professor is far more likely to become well known and respected in his or
her field from publishing than from being an exceptional teacher. In fact,
I can't think of a single person in my field who developed a national reputation based solely on the excellence of his or her teaching. Furthermore,
colleges are far more likely to reward faculty who are scholars with merit
salary increases, sabbaticals, travel funds, released time, and other perks
than they are ones who are exceptional teachers.

That said, I believe a case can also be made for this assumption being
questionable. I am 68 years old and have been employed in academia for
37 years. I've had more than 150 articles and 22 books published. I am a
Fellow of the two academic/professional associations to which I belong and
am listed in *Who's Who in America* and a number of other national and
international academic/professional biographical volumes. I've received several awards for my research and publications including a "Nobel"-type
prize for my research on rehabilitation that was funded by the Royal Family
of Saudi Arabia. However, when I think back over my career about what
has given me the most pleasure (i.e., from what I've received the most long-
lasting payoffs) it has been the students with whom I've been privileged to
interact during my years in academia. If I continue to impact professionally
10 years after I retire, it's more likely to be through my students than
through my research and publications. (My publications, incidentally, are
probably more likely to continue to impact professionally 10 years after I
retire than they would otherwise because my students are likely to continue
to advocate some of my positions.) Consequently, while the short-term,
tangible payoffs from being successful as a scholar are likely to exceed those
from teaching well, it will not necessarily be true for the long-term, intan-
gible ones if you are willing to invest in teaching well. Your legacy to your

field 10 years after you retire is more likely to be your students than your articles and books (particularly if they aren't printed on acid-free paper)!

POTENTIAL BENEFITS AND LOSSES FROM INVESTING IN TEACHING

Pursuing any activity requires an investment of time, energy, possibly money, and a willingness to be uncomfortable. And the benefits you derive may or may not exceed the losses you're likely to incur. Consequently, the probable benefit–loss ratio may not be sufficiently favorable to make the activity worth pursuing. Teaching is no exception. In this section, we will consider some of the variables that can affect the benefit–loss ratio for investing in teaching.

The benefits you may receive by investing sufficiently in teaching to do it well include the following:

- A reduction in the likelihood that questions will be raised about your teaching, particularly if you attempt to be promoted and tenured before your "up or out" year.
- A lessening of the opportunity for your chairperson and others to use teaching as an excuse for denying you tenure when the real reason is something that they would have a difficult time documenting otherwise (e.g., a perceived lack of collegiality).
- A reputation as a good teacher, thereby, for example, increasing the likelihood of your having an adequate enrollment for elective courses (including summer session ones that will be canceled if the enrollment is too small).
- Enjoyment from knowing that you are doing something well.
- A greater understanding of your field (one of the best ways to learn something is to teach it).
- Teaching awards from your institution and/or professional association(s).
- More opportunities to collaborate with both undergraduate and graduate students on publishable research projects.
- Ideas for publishable research projects from conversations with individual students and class discussions.
- Opportunities to author textbooks (based on your courses) and other educational materials.
- More graduate students.
- Extra income from invitations to present continuing education courses and workshops.
- A greater likelihood that your points of view will continue to impact on your field long after you retire and your publications turn to dust.

Of course, there are probably other ways as well that you could benefit from teaching well.

Unfortunately, the potential consequences of investing significantly in teaching are not all desirable. Doing so can have undesirable ones, including the following:

• Having less time available for research and publication.
• Having less time available for grant writing.
• Having to cope with your colleagues being envious and jealous because of your good relationships with students.
• Becoming depressed because your students do not appear to appreciate you as a teacher and/or the "sacrifices" you've made to teach them well.

This list is unlikely to be exhaustive.

Any benefit–loss ratio you compute for investing in teaching should be regarded as being an *approximation* (i.e., tentative) since it was based on the information you had when you computed it. As you become more aware of the potential benefits and losses from investing in teaching and are better able to accurately assign weights to them, the values you compute for this ratio will more closely approximate the true one, assuming, of course, that its true value remains constant. This, unfortunately, isn't a safe assumption to make because the benefits you are likely to derive from teaching well probably will not remain constant throughout your academic career. Nor will the benefits you are likely to derive from publication and grant writing. In spite of these limitations, periodically doing the soul-searching needed to compute this ratio will tend to increase the likelihood that your teaching record will be adequate for promotion and tenure.

QUALITY EXPECTATIONS FOR TEACHING IN PROMOTION AND TENURE DECISIONS

These expectations vary somewhat depending on:

• The value that the department and the institution place on teaching well.
• The amount of confidence in their ability to document deficiencies in teaching well enough to defend against a legal challenge.
• The dedication of the members of the departmental, college, and university promotion and tenure committees to teaching.
• The strength of a candidate's publication and grant-funding records.
• Whether a candidate is seeking promotion and tenure before his or her "up or out" year.
• How difficult a candidate would be to replace.
• The strength of the department's desire to deny a candidate tenure.

Each of these is dealt with in this section.

The Value That the Department and the Institution Place on Teaching Well

This will vary depending on how the department and the institution define their mission. All departments and institutions, of course, expect teaching to meet at least minimal quality standards. Probably the only acceptable excuses for failing to meet them would be being a well-known public figure (e.g., a former president of the United States) or attracting millions of dollars in grant funding. Most departments would be willing to excuse a person who did the latter from teaching undergraduates.

Departments in two-year community colleges and in private four-year liberal arts colleges tend to define their primary mission as teaching and their primary requirement for tenure as teaching well. There may be departments at such an institution, however, in which considerable weight tends to be given to publication in promotion and tenure decisions. Be aware that the number of such departments appears to be increasing, even in two-year community colleges.

The departments that tend to give the least weight to teaching in promotion and tenure decisions are ones at large universities that offer the Ph.D. degree and have a strong commitment to research, particularly funded research. While publication and success in grant writing in such departments tend to be given more weight than teaching in promotion and tenure decisions, they nevertheless expect their faculty to teach reasonably well. A faculty member in such a department who teaches poorly is unlikely to be tenured unless he or she brings in huge amounts of grant funding.

The Amount of Confidence in Their Ability to Document Deficiencies in Teaching Well Enough to Defend Against a Legal Challenge

It's no longer highly unusual for faculty who are denied tenure to at least threaten to challenge the decision in court. Consequently, many colleges and universities would hesitate denying tenure solely for this reason unless they were able to document adequately both deficiencies in teaching and attempts to assist the faculty member to remedy them.

The Dedication of the Members of the Departmental, College, and University Promotion and Tenure Committees to Teaching

A candidate's record for promotion and tenure is adequate if those judging it deem it to be adequate. Likewise, it is inadequate if they deem it to be so. The weight that a member of a promotion and tenure committee gives a candidate's teaching record is influenced by the weight that he or she gives the candidate's publication and grant-writing records. Consequently, the teaching record of a candidate who has a strong publication and/or grant-writing record could be regarded as adequate by a committee member who gives considerable weight to publication and/or grant writing and inadequate by one who doesn't.

An assistant professor is unlikely to know in advance the biases of all those who will be judging his or her application for promotion and tenure. Consequently, he or she would be wise to invest sufficiently in teaching to amass a record that almost anybody would be likely to deem adequate.

The Strength of a Candidate's Publication and Grant-Funding Records

A candidate who has a strong publication and/or grant-funding record is likely at almost any college or university to have more deficiencies in teaching excused than one who doesn't, as long as these deficiencies do not reach the level of constituting poor teaching. Few department chairpersons would relish the thought of having to deal with student complaints about a member of their department's teaching for the remainder of their tenure as chairperson, regardless of how strong a national reputation the faculty member had as a scholar or how much extramural funding he or she brought in.

Whether a Candidate Is Seeking Promotion and Tenure Before His or Her "Up or Out" Year

Promotion and tenure committee members tend to have a different standard for judging the adequacy of a candidate's teaching record if he or she asks to be considered for promotion and tenure before the "up or out" year. They are likely to vote to deny it if there is any question about the adequacy of the candidate's teaching, even if he or she has a strong publication and extramural funding record. Their reasoning is that by doing so they are likely to motivate the candidate to try to improve the adequacy of his or her teaching before again asking to be considered for promotion and tenure. Consequently, if there is a possibility that you'll be seeking promotion and tenure before the end of your probationary period, it is crucial that your teacher ratings and other documentation pertaining to your teaching indicate unequivocally that it's more than adequate.

How Difficult a Candidate Would Be to Replace

If your field is one in which there is a shortage of Ph.D.'s interested in college teaching, deficiencies in your teaching that don't rise to the level of making you a poor teacher may be excused because the answer to the question "Can we do better?" would be likely to be, "No." It would be extremely risky, however, to count on this happening because the availability of Ph.D.'s for teaching positions in all fields can vary considerably from year to year.

The Strength of the Department's Desire to Deny a Candidate Tenure

A candidate's department may not support him or her for promotion and tenure. There could be a number of reasons including deficiencies in scholarship (i.e., research and publication), grant writing, teaching, and/or collegiality. The latter, in my experience, was frequently the real reason for the majority of the tenured faculty in a department not supporting an assistant professor for promotion and tenure. They apparently perceived the person as being unwilling to do his or her fair share of committee work and student advising and/or as being a chronic complainer or troublemaker.

If the chairperson and senior faculty in a department strongly desire to deny a candidate tenure, one way that they may attempt to do it is by questioning the quality of his or her teaching. They are particularly likely to use teaching if the candidate's ratings from students are on the low side. The chairperson and senior faculty may question the quality of the candidate's teaching in the letters they write for his or her promotion and tenure document and/or they may ask students who they know consider the candidate to be a poor teacher to write letters for it.

TEACHING CREATIVELY CAN FACILITATE PUBLISHING FOR TENURE

An adequate publishing record is also required for promotion and tenure (see Silverman, 1999). Teaching creatively can help to generate such a record. Some of the types of publications that teaching creatively can yield are described in this section.

Articles on Innovative Approaches to Teaching

Articles of this type can be a particularly good source for publications in fields that don't tend to be experimental ones, such as those in the humanities and fine arts (e.g., theater). There are journals that peer-review submissions in most such fields that will publish such articles.

Reports about innovative approaches to teaching can also be presented at professional association conventions as either poster or platform presentations. Such presentations, incidentally, are likely to attract a larger "audience" than ones that report research findings.

Textbooks

Part or all of the content and organization of a course that you teach well and/or innovatively can be communicated in printed or electronic form as a textbook. Opportunities for authoring textbooks exist in all fields. For practical information about textbook authoring and publishing, see Silverman (1998).

A textbook you author that is widely adopted and based, at least in part, on a course that you teach can be used to help make the case that you teach well. Since college teachers tend to base the organization and content of their courses largely on the textbooks they use, it can be argued that if your course wasn't a good one, a book based on it probably wouldn't have been widely adopted.

Be aware, however, that non-tenured faculty in some departments and at some institutions can be harmed by authoring textbooks. These are likely to be departments or institutions that expect faculty to pursue extramural grant funding. While such funding is given to the institution, royalty income from textbooks is given to their authors. Consequently, departments and institutions benefit directly financially from faculty efforts at grant funding but not from faculty efforts at textbook authoring. You would be wise, therefore, to find out whether your department or institution discourages textbook authoring by junior faculty before contracting to write one.

Collaborative Student/Faculty Research Projects

If the students in your department respect you as a teacher, they are more likely to gravitate to you for directing their master's theses and doctoral dissertations. If the idea for such a project is yours or if you contribute significantly to it in another way, you can co-author an article in a peer-reviewed journal based on it with the student and/or do a joint poster or platform presentation with him or her at a professional association meeting.

If the students in your department respect you as a teacher, they are also more likely to be interested in participating in your research projects. They could, for example, help you to gather data, thereby making it easier for you to complete publishable projects.

BEING HATED BY STUDENTS IS NEITHER COMFORTABLE NOR SURVIVAL ENHANCING

Our primary focus thus far in this chapter has been on the importance of teaching well for achieving promotion and tenure. You may be at an institution in or a department that tends to give very little weight to teaching when making promotion and tenure decisions. At such an institution or in such a department it may be possible to be promoted and tenured even if you are a mediocre teacher. You may even get substantial merit salary increases and achieve a national reputation as a scholar if you are one. Why, then, might it be worthwhile for you to invest, at least a little, in learning to teach well?

Most of us like to be liked and, consequently, would find it uncomfortable having to interact at our workplace almost every day with persons who dislike us. Those of us who have at least a little tendency to be perfectionistic would find having to do so particularly uncomfortable. If you don't care enough about your students to try to teach well, many (perhaps most) of them will be aware of it and they will dislike you for valuing them so little. They could communicate their dislike in a number of ways including giving you low teacher ratings, writing negative letters for your promotion and tenure document, complaining about you to your chairperson or dean, and/or refusing to enroll in courses you teach that aren't required ones.

2

Approaches Used to Evaluate Teaching for Tenure

The objective assessment of teaching adequacy for tenure can be (and usually is) a highly subjective process for at least two reasons:

- There is a lack of agreement about what constitutes good teaching in higher education.
- The validity, reliability, and generality of the data that both have been and are likely to continue being used to evaluate teaching are uncertain.

Yet, there can be almost universal agreement about whether a particular individual is a good teacher or a poor one. Some implications of these conclusions, particularly for persons seeking tenure, are indicated in this chapter.

WHAT CONSTITUTES GOOD TEACHING IN HIGHER EDUCATION?

A necessary condition for determining how close a goal is to being achieved is being able to define how someone who has achieved it both would and would not behave. Consequently, a necessary condition for determining how well a candidate for tenure is teaching is being able to define how someone would behave who is regarded as being a great teacher or an extremely poor one—the extremes on the teaching quality continuum. While there have been many attempts to define what constitutes good teaching at the college level, there is no consensus regarding a set of criteria for judging its presence and absence. Yet, students and others appear to believe that they are able to recognize both.

Perhaps we can glean a little insight into how a teacher would behave who is regarded as being at the upper end of the teaching quality continuum from the responses of a group of Marquette University alumni (published in a 1999 issue of the university's alumni magazine) to the following question: "What makes a great teacher?" The following comments were abstracted from them:

- "A willingness to share knowledge, an inspirational love for learning, and a real respect for students."
- "A teacher's wisdom, however, is not expressed simply in his or her command of the subject. . . . It is also shown in the way a teacher seeks the truth, inspires students to learn, and teaches the life lessons that students remember long after exams and term papers are completed."
- "A sense of humor, dynamic methods of presenting ideas and information, a passion for learning, an example of hard work."
- "Great teachers show their constant abiding respect for the fundamental dignity of their students in every gesture, glance, expression."
- "The difference between a good teacher and a great teacher is the word 'compassion.' "
- "Being extremely knowledgeable on the subjects taught, clear, concise, and well organized."
- "Instilling in students a sense of hard work, diligence, responsibility, and a can-do attitude."
- "Sharing their love of knowledge and inspiring their students to pursue it also."
- "Setting high standards of students and having a knack for leading them to their goals."
- Seeking out students, both those who are very gifted and may need the additional push to take advantage of their gifts and those who need help but are unwilling to step forward on their own to seek it."
- "Teaching a desert-dry subject in a way that makes it so interesting and thought-provoking to students that they will explore it on their own."

Note that these characteristics go considerably beyond being knowledgeable about what one teaches and teaching it clearly.

How would a teacher behave who functions at the other end of this continuum? Based on these comments, he or she would communicate to students that he or she didn't respect them in a number of ways, including not preparing adequately for classes. And they would probably reciprocate by giving him or her low ratings for teaching.

You don't have to be a great teacher to be tenured—just a good one. Nevertheless, you are likely to find it rewarding to become one for reasons other than being tenured (see Chapter 1).

THE ROLE OF THE OBSERVER AND THE OBSERVED IN JUDGING TEACHING ADEQUACY

Albert Einstein pointed out many years ago that the world as we know it is the product of an interaction between the observer and the observed. Two persons who observe an event are highly unlikely to perceive it exactly the same way because of differences in their experiences, expectations, biases, and so on. There is, therefore, no objective reality for the labels "poor," "adequate," or "great" teaching. Consequently, it is more appropriate to inquire whether a professor's teaching *is perceived as* adequate for being tenured than to inquire whether his or her teaching *is* adequate for being so.

Just as the students who have taken a course are unlikely to agree with each other about how well the course was taught, their own judgment about how well it was taught may change. What they considered to be good teaching at the end of the course, they may no longer regard as having been good teaching five years after they graduate, and vice versa.

It is crucial for a professor's mental health that he or she constantly keep in mind that the judgments students and others make about his or her teaching are perhaps as much about them as they are about his or her teaching. In this regard, I taught a course a number of years ago in which student comments at the end ranged from "the best professor I ever had" to "the only way to improve this course would be to fire the professor."

Fortunately, some (perhaps most) of the factors that tend to influence judgments of teaching adequacy have been identified. A number of strategies are described elsewhere in the book for manipulating them in ways that are likely to result in your teaching being judged to be at least adequate.

HOW COLLEGES AND UNIVERSITIES JUDGE TEACHING

The data that the members of a promotion and tenure committee utilize for assessing the adequacy of a candidate's teaching could come from one or more of the following:

- Student rating forms and analyses thereof
- Letters from students
- Student interviews
- "Underground" student publications giving course recommendations
- An evaluation letter from the chairperson and possibly also the dean
- Letters from department faculty and others at the institution and possibly also from other institutions where the candidate taught
- A departmental promotion and tenure committee report

- A college promotion and tenure committee report
- A self-evaluation of strengths and weaknesses
- Content of course syllabi
- Colleague ratings based on classroom visits
- Evaluations of videotapes of classroom teaching
- Teaching outside of the classroom
- Alumni opinions
- Teaching improvement activities
- Popularity of elective courses
- Development of courses for emerging areas
- Student performance on external examinations
- Long-term follow-up of how alumni perform
- Teaching-related awards and grants received
- Invitations to lecture and/or present workshops at other institutions or at meetings of professional associations
- Textbooks and other teaching materials authored and adoptions thereof
- Articles and convention presentations that describe innovative approaches to teaching

There, of course, could be other types of data that promotion and tenure members would consider relevant for assessing teaching adequacy. Some possible implications of using each of them for this purpose are indicated in this section.

Student Rating Forms and Analyses Thereof

These are among the most frequently used types of data for assessing teaching adequacy for tenure. Some departments, including mine, require them to be administered at the end of every course you teach in which there are at least five students.

The students in a class are asked to rate their instructor on a number of numerical scales. The ratings they assign to each scale are averaged. The average of the average ratings for the set of scales is also likely to be computed. These averages are given considerable weight when judging teaching adequacy because they reflect the judgments of the group of people who, at least theoretically, know best how well the course was taught because they were there.

The students may be asked to judge their instructor in other ways as well. They may, for example, be given a list of words and phrases and asked to place a check mark beside those that describe him or her. The list may include some or all of the following: well-prepared, ineffective, lenient, hard to understand, competent, good sense of humor, unfriendly, fair/unbiased, effective, understandable, cold, ill-prepared, boring, confident, biased/one-sided, poor sense-of-humor, nervous, stimulating, friendly, warm, hostile, sloppy, interesting, and incompetent. The percentage of students who place a check mark beside each may be computed. In addition, they may be asked to compare the difficulty of the course to others they have taken, to indicate the recommendation they would give a friend about taking the course, and to give an overall rating of the instructor.

There has been considerable research on the validity, reliability, and generality of the data yielded by such forms. Both this research and some issues pertaining to the use of such data for promotion and tenure decisions are dealt with in Chapter 3.

Letters from Students

At many institutions (including mine), letters from students are routinely included in applications for promotion and tenure. The number, based on my experience, can be as few as two or as many as 25. Students who are asked to submit letters are likely to be ones who have been randomly selected from a "population" consisting of persons who have taken at least one of the candidate's courses. Such letters could also include unsolicited ones from students containing comments on the candidate's teaching that had been sent to the candidate or to his or her chairperson or dean. Incidentally, if you receive any letters from students in which they say nice things about your teaching, you'd be wise to send copies to both your chairperson and dean and ask that they be included in your promotion and tenure dossier (unless, of course, there is a good reason for not doing so, such as professional envy or jealousy).

Members of promotion and tenure committees may scan student letters for at least two kinds of information. The first is reservations about the adequacy of a candidate's teaching. Such reservations may either be stated or can be inferred from comments that were (or possibly were not) made. The more motivated a committee member is to deny a candidate tenure, the more likely he or she is to scan student letters for the latter. Even a single negative comment from a good student can cause the adequacy of the candidate's teaching to be questioned, particularly if the positive comments by other students tend to be lukewarm.

The second type of information for which such letters may be scanned is their consistency with other data about a candidate's teaching (e.g., his or her student ratings). If the impression committee members get from the letters is consistent with what they get from other sources, it is likely to increase the confidence they have in their judgment about the adequacy of a candidate's teaching.

Student Interviews

These may be interviews that are conducted specifically for gathering information about a candidate's teaching or that are conducted for another purpose from which such information can be gleaned. An example of the latter would be exit interviews of graduating seniors that are conducted routinely by the chairpersons of some departments. It's not unusual for comments to be made about the teaching of individual professors during such interviews.

Interviews conducted specifically for gathering information about a candidate's teaching may be either informal or formal. An example of an informal interview would be a member of a departmental promotion and tenure committee informally questioning a few students who were in his or her office for another reason about the candidate's teaching. He or she would probably communicate the information obtained orally (not in writing) to the other members of the committee, perhaps at one of their meetings. An example of a formal interview would be one in which individual students or small groups of students would be questioned by the members of a promotion and tenure committee about the adequacy of a candidate's teaching and their answers to questions and comments would be recorded and communicated in a written report.

Student interviews that are specifically intended to gather information about a candidate's teaching tend to be time-consuming and, consequently, are unlikely to be conducted routinely. They're most likely to be conducted when serious questions have been raised about the adequacy of a candidate's teaching. Persons who are denied tenure for this reason may sue the institution and formal reports of such interviews (or depositions from students who participated in them) can be helpful to the attorneys who are representing the institution in such litigation.

"Underground" Student Publications Giving Course Recommendations

Students on some campuses distribute booklets in which they evaluate courses and instructors. Comments from such publications are unlikely to be included routinely in applications for promotion and tenure. A candidate may find it advantageous, however, to request that such comments be included if they are all (or almost all) favorable.

An Evaluation Letter from the Chairperson and Possibly Also the Dean

Almost all dossiers for promotion and tenure contain a letter from the candidate's chairperson and possibly also his or her dean. About the only circumstance in which there would not be a letter from the chairperson is when the candidate is the chairperson.

The chairperson's letter will contain an evaluation of the candidate's service to the department (and possibly also to the institution and profession), his or her research, and teaching. With respect to teaching, the letter is likely to provide committee members with some insight into how the chairperson, the students, and the majority of the department's faculty regard its adequacy.

If a chairperson questions the adequacy of a candidate's teaching, members of the committee will be seeking a clear statement of why he or she is doing so. The weight that they give the letter will be determined, in large part, by how troublesome and well documented they regard the concerns spoken about in it.

If a candidate's teacher ratings throughout his or her probationary period were relatively low, members of the committee probably will be seeking documentation in the chairperson's report for the candidate having been told repeatedly to improve his or her teaching and for efforts being made to help him or her to do so. If this hadn't been done, the candidate would have a valid reason for believing that his or her teaching was deemed to be adequate in spite of his or her relatively low teacher ratings. Consequently, the members of the committee could consider it unfair to begin questioning its adequacy at the end of the probationary period and to refuse to deny tenure for this reason. They would be particularly likely to do so if a candidate had a strong publication and/or grant procurement record.

A letter from the dean may also be included in the dossier. It is particularly likely to be given considerable weight by the members of the committee if the department chairperson is very negative about the candidate in his or her letter and the dean believes that the reason is a personality conflict and/or professional envy or jealousy, at least in part.

Letters from Department Faculty and Others at the Institution and Possibly Also from Other Institutions Where the Candidate Taught

The faculty members of the candidate's department are likely to be asked to write letters for the dossier. Others at the institution and elsewhere may also be asked to do so. Those from outside the department and institution probably would have had their names given to the person assembling the dossier by the candidate.

Some of the letters may not deal with the candidate's teaching or do so only superficially. That is, their primary focus may be his or her contributions as a scholar, grantsmanship, and/or collegiality, rather than teaching.

Negative comments about a candidate in even one such letter that don't appear to be motivated by professional envy or jealousy and/or a personality conflict can place his or her bid for tenure "at risk." They are particularly likely to do so if the candidate is seeking tenure before his or her "up or out" year.

A Departmental Promotion and Tenure Committee Report

Some departments have a promotion and tenure committee. A person seeking tenure in such a department would be considered by it before being considered by the college and/or university one. A report containing the committee's vote on granting the person tenure (with or without promotion) and their reasons for voting as they did would be added to his or her dossier before it is considered by the college and/or university promotion and tenure committee(s).

A person whose bid for tenure wasn't supported by the majority of the departmental committee may decide against having his or her dossier considered by the college and/or university committee(s). He or she may either delay having it considered for a year or two (assuming that it wasn't the person's "up or out" year) or resign. The person's prospects for getting another college teaching position are likely to be better if he or she resigns before the end of the probationary period than if he or she is fired at the end of it for not performing well enough to be tenured.

A College Promotion and Tenure Committee Report

The candidate's college is likely to have a committee that will evaluate his or her dossier. They will draft a report that gives their vote for granting the person tenure (with or without promotion) and their reasons for voting as they did. This report will be added to the dossier. The dossier may then have to be considered and voted on by a university promotion and tenure committee.

At some colleges and universities (including mine) votes by promotion and tenure committees are considered to be advisory. Tenure decisions are made by the vice president for academic affairs or by another upper-level administrator. It isn't highly unusual at such institutions for someone who isn't supported for tenure by one or more of the promotion and tenure committees who evaluated his or her dossier to be tenured and vice versa.

A Self-Evaluation of Strengths and Weaknesses

A candidate for tenure may be asked to prepare a self-evaluation of teaching for the dossier. He or she is expected to identify shortcomings and to indicate what has been and will be done to correct them.

Such self-evaluations can provide at least two kinds of useful information. First, they can provide information about how well the person's judgment of his or her teaching quality agrees with that of students and others. A person whose teaching isn't particularly good but fails to acknowledge a need to improve it is unlikely to do so. And second, it can provide information about the person's awareness of specific shortcomings and what he or she has done and may do in the future to correct them. A person going up for tenure in the "up or out" year who shows signs of being aware of the need to improve his or her teaching, appears to know what has to be done to do so, and has begun doing it, is less likely to be denied tenure for this reason, particularly if the person also has a strong publication and/or grantsmanship record.

Content of Course Syllabi

The inclusion of course syllabi in the dossier may be mandatory or optional. They can provide information about what topics are covered, how up-to-date the presentation is, and the willingness of the person to at least mention widely accepted points-of view with which he or she disagrees. They can also provide information about the degree to which the person's teaching is innovative and his or her use of the Internet and other electronic media for instructional purposes.

Course syllabi are unlikely to be mentioned as a reason for denying tenure unless the courses a person teaches are required ones in which certain topics have to be dealt with and the person refuses to deal with some of them. The person may refuse to do so because they aren't a part of his or her specialty. If certain topics have to be covered in a course and you feel that you lack the knowledge needed to teach some of them, it's your responsibility to acquire the necessary knowledge. Your refusal to do so would be a legitimate reason for denying you tenure. Nobody expects you to be an authority on everything you teach!

Colleague Ratings Based on Classroom Visits

It is customary, in some departments, for the dossier to contain at least one report on the person's teaching that was drafted by a colleague who sat in on several classes. In others, such classroom visits are only made when there appears to be a problem. Their main purpose is almost always to help the person improve his or her teaching rather than evaluate it.

Assistant professors whose student teacher ratings tend to be relatively low might find it advantageous to request such a visit. They could conceivably benefit in at least two ways. First, the suggestions made may enable them to improve their teaching. And second, the fact that they requested such a visit is likely to be construed as evidence that they are attempting to improve it.

Evaluations of Videotapes of Classroom Teaching

Such evaluations can provide the same kinds of data as do classroom visits if someone other than the candidate decides which classes are to be videotaped. They have the advantage of being less intrusive than classroom visits and the potential to be evaluated more thoroughly than them because a videotape can be viewed more than once by any number of colleagues.

Teaching Outside of the Classroom

An example of such teaching would be directing student research. Departments tend to value highly this type of involvement with students, particularly if it results in publications. Another example of such teaching would be practicum supervision. Letters from students who feel strongly that they have benefited from interacting with you in such a way can be helpful both for making the case that you're interested in teaching and for documenting that your teaching is at least adequate.

Alumni Opinions

It has been argued that people may not be able to judge accurately how well they've been taught until after they graduate. There could be at least two reasons. First, they may not be able to judge the adequacy of the knowledge and skills they acquired until they're on the job. And second, they may not have an opportunity before they graduate to compare their knowledge and skills with those of persons who were trained elsewhere.

There are at least a few letters from alumni in most dossiers for promotion and tenure. You may be asked by the person preparing your dossier for a list of alumni to contact. Consequently, you may want to begin putting together a list of names and addresses of both students who appear to like your teaching and alumni who have told you that your teaching was helpful to them.

Teaching Improvement Activities

These include attending professional/academic conventions, participating in formal continuing education activities (e.g., courses and workshops), regularly reading print and electronic journals, and periodically "surfing the Internet" for material that's relevant to your courses. They can also include having your teaching critiqued and attempting to correct weaknesses.

Less than adequate teaching may be forgiven if the person appears to be making a real effort to improve. Doing all of the above would likely be regarded as compelling evidence that the person is making such an effort.

Popularity of Elective Courses

Everything else being equal, good teachers tend to attract more students to their elective courses than do poor ones. Relatively large enrollments in such courses can be used as evidence of teaching adequacy, particularly if the courses are regarded as being challenging (rather than easy) and/or aren't ones that students feel compelled to take even though they are electives.

Relatively low enrollments in elective courses can indicate poor teaching, but there can also be a number of other explanations. Students, for example, may be limited in the number of electives that they can take and may view the content of others as being more relevant to their needs. Or an elective may be offered at a time when few students can fit it into their schedule.

Perhaps the best scenario for the enrollment in an elective being considered compelling evidence for good teaching is the course consistently attracting large numbers of non-majors as well as majors and consistently getting high ratings from students.

Development of Courses for Emerging Areas

The voluntary development of a course needed to make one's students competent in an emerging area would be indicative of a genuine interest in teaching. It would be particularly so if the course was one of the first to be developed for the area. Such a course, incidentally, could provide both the organization and some of the content for a textbook. This was how the first edition of a textbook I authored (Silverman, 1995) that is currently in its third edition came to be written.

Student Performance on External Examinations

One of the more objective indices that have been used to gauge teaching adequacy is student performance on examinations administered by groups that aren't affiliated with the person's college or university, such as ones for certification and licensure. It sometimes is possible with such examinations to get feedback about the areas in which those taking them appear to be particularly weak. If one or more such areas were ones for which the person seeking tenure was responsible, it would not reflect particularly well on the adequacy of his or her teaching.

Long-Term Follow-Up of How Alumni Perform

Some departments that train professionals (including mine) survey persons who employ or supervise their students a few years after they graduate to determine how satisfied they are with their performance on the job. Comments about their knowledge and skills in a particular area could reflect either positively or negatively on the adequacy of the courses taught by a particular faculty member.

Teaching-Related Awards and Grants Received

The receipt of an award for teaching from the department, institution, or a professional association would probably be regarded as compelling evidence that the recipient has been performing at least adequately as a teacher. And the receipt of a teaching-related grant would probably be regarded as compelling evidence that the recipient is genuinely interested in teaching and tends to be innovative in how he or she does it.

Invitations to Lecture and/or Present Workshops at Other Institutions or at Meetings of Professional Associations

Such invitations, particularly if they are repeat ones, suggest that the person has a reputation as being at least an adequate teacher.

Textbooks and Other Teaching Materials Authored and Adoptions Thereof

The authoring of textbooks or other teaching materials usually indicates a genuine interest in teaching. If they are based on or from courses a person teaches and are widely adopted, this obviously says something about the quality of the courses.

Articles and Convention Presentations That Describe Innovative Approaches to Teaching

Such articles and convention presentations indicate a genuine interest in teaching. They also suggest that the person is striving to teach more effectively.

RECOGNIZING GOOD TEACHING IS LIKE RECOGNIZING A FACE

It's difficult to define what constitutes good teaching. Yet good teaching isn't particularly difficult to recognize. Perhaps what enables us to recognize it is what Michael Polanyi (1967) has referred to as "tacit knowing." According to Polanyi, *we can know more than we can tell.* This fact seems obvious enough; but it is not easy to say exactly what it means. Take an example. We know a person's face and can recognize it among a thousand, indeed among a million. Yet we usually cannot tell how we recognize a face we know. (Polanyi, 1967, p. 4)

The phenomenon of tacit knowing provides some justification for arguing that it is possible for a person to recognize adequate and inadequate teaching even if the person isn't consciously aware of how he or she does it.

WHAT YOU CAN DO TO MAXIMIZE THE LIKELIHOOD THAT YOUR TEACHING WILL BE CONSIDERED AT LEAST ADEQUATE

To survive well in academia, you must be regarded by students and others (through tacit knowing) as being at least an adequate teacher. While there is no universally accepted definition for what constitutes good teaching, some of the variables that influence judgments of teaching adequacy have been identified. My main focus in this book is on strategies for manipulating these variables to yield teacher ratings from students and others that are likely to be high enough to be tenured.

3

Student Ratings of Teaching

Student ratings, as I've indicated previously, are among the types of data that are used most frequently for making teaching-related tenure decisions. They are also the measure of teaching adequacy at the college level about which we have the most information concerning validity, reliability, generality, and the impact of extraneous variables (Cashin, 1995). Some research findings concerning each of these will be summarized in this chapter.*

VALIDITY

Do student ratings of teaching really measure what they are supposed to measure? That is, are the items that usually appear on teaching rating forms really aspects of teaching effectiveness, and do students have the opportunity and experience to make the observations and judgments needed to rate them? These questions are difficult to answer definitively because, as I've indicated previously, there is no generally accepted definition of teaching effectiveness. That said, there is considerable agreement on the appropriateness of a few criteria for judging teaching effectiveness. These include student learning, instructor's self-ratings, administrator's ratings, colleague's ratings, and student responses to open-ended questions. Some of the data relevant to the relationship (correlation) between each of these criteria and student ratings of teaching are summarized in this section.

---

*My primary source for this chapter was Cashin (1995). It contains an excellent bibliography for initiating a search of this literature.

Students' Ability to Recognize Good Teaching

Students would have to know what constitutes good teaching for their ratings to be valid. There have been a number of studies in which students' views of what constitutes good teaching have been compared to that of faculty. The findings of these studies suggest that what students consider good teaching is very similar to what faculty consider good teaching. Consequently, assuming that most faculty know what constitutes good teaching, most students do also.

Student Learning

The primary role of a college teacher is to facilitate student learning. Consequently, a valid criterion for assessing teaching effectiveness would be the amount that students learn. Other things being equal, students should learn more from a relatively effective teacher than from one who is relatively ineffective.

There have been a number of studies in which students in multisection courses that were taught by different instructors with the same syllabus and textbook were given a final examination that was developed by someone other than the instructors. Their scores on the examination were correlated with their teaching ratings. The results were consistent with the premise that student teaching ratings are valid because the sections in which the students gave their instructors the highest ratings were also the ones in which they tended to score the highest on the examination.

Instructor's Self-Ratings

A college teacher would usually know which of two courses he or she taught most effectively. There have been several studies in which the way that an instructor would rank order two or more courses on the basis of how effectively they were taught was compared to a rank order based on student ratings. Both rank orderings in these studies were very similar, thereby providing additional support for student ratings being valid.

Administrators' and Colleagues' Ratings

There have been a number of studies in which administrators' and colleagues' ratings of teaching were correlated with those of students. Assuming that chairpersons and colleagues know how well faculty in their department teach, the findings of most of these studies tend to support the premise that student ratings are valid.

Trained Observers

There have been studies in which the global teaching ratings of trained observers based on classroom observation were compared to those of students. The judgments of the trained observers in most of these studies were similar to those of the students, thereby providing additional support for student ratings of teaching being valid.

Student Responses to Open-Ended Questions

Student's evaluations of teaching based on their responses to open-ended questions have been compared to ones based on their ratings. The judgments of teaching adequacy yielded by both methods in these studies were very similar. Consequently, if you consider judgments of teaching adequacy based on responses to open-ended questions to be valid data, you would have to consider those based on ratings to be so also.

RELIABILITY

Two types of measures of interrater agreement have been used to determine whether student teaching ratings are sufficiently reliable for assessing teaching adequacy. The first indicates whether the students in a class agree well enough with each other on the ratings they assign the items on the rating sheet for the means of their ratings to yield reliable measures of what the items are intended to measure. The second indicates how stable the ratings given to a particular instructor in a particular course tend to remain over time (assuming, of course, that both the content of the course and how it is taught do not change significantly from semester to semester).

With regard to the first of these measures, the research indicates unequivocally that the reliability of such ratings is, in part, a function of the number of raters. The more raters, the more reliable both the means for individual items and the overall mean (i.e., the mean of the means for the various items). The research also indicates that data from courses in which at least 10 students complete the rating form should be sufficiently reliable for judging teaching adequacy and the reliability of that from ratings of fewer than 10 students is uncertain. Such data should be interpreted with particular caution if based on ratings from fewer than six students.

With regard to the second of these measures, the research tends to indicate that the ratings students give an instructor for a particular course usually vary little from semester to semester. Furthermore, there is some evidence that the ratings students give a course a year or so after they graduate vary little from those they gave it at the end. Consequently, student ratings appear to be sufficiently stable for judging how well a particular course tends to be taught.

GENERALITY

To judge teaching adequacy for tenure, data are needed that accurately reflect an instructor's general teaching effectiveness, rather than how effective he or she taught a particular course a particular semester. The research suggests that ratings from a single course are unlikely to be adequate for this purpose. While the ratings that an instructor receives from the students in a particular course may vary little from semester to semester, those that the instructor usually receive in the various courses he or she teaches can vary considerably. I have taught six courses for the past 25 years and the ratings that I've received from students have consistently been higher in some than in others. Consequently, to adequately judge an instructor's general teaching effectiveness, you need student ratings from all of the courses the instructor taught, particularly the ones that he or she taught during the previous two years.

EXTRANEOUS VARIABLES THAT DO AND DO NOT APPEAR TO SIGNIFICANTLY AFFECT STUDENT RATINGS (AS WELL AS OTHER JUDGMENTS) OF TEACHING

What variables can influence the ratings that students give a course other than how well it is taught? A number of variables have been alleged to have this ability. The relevant research suggests that some of them are highly likely to bias student ratings, at least a little, and others are not. The findings for some such variables are summarized here.

Variables That *May* Be Extraneous to Teaching That Can Affect Student Ratings

Prior Interest in the Subject Matter

Students tend to give higher ratings to an instructor if they had a prior interest in the subject matter that was dealt with in a course. They would, therefore, tend to give higher ratings to instructors of courses in their major and minor than they would to others.

Their reason for giving an instructor higher ratings when they had a prior interest in the subject matter dealt with in his or her course may be related to the amount that they learned. When students have a prior interest in the subject matter dealt with in a course, they are likely to be more highly motivated to learn. Consequently, their tendency to rate their instructor a little higher may merely reflect the fact that they learned more than they would have otherwise.

Reason for Taking the Course

Students tend to give higher teaching ratings to instructors of electives than to those of required courses. This could, of course, merely reflect the fact that they tend to be more interested in learning what is taught in electives than in required courses and, consequently, invest more of themselves in doing so. The more a student learns in a course, the more highly he or she is likely to rate the instructor who taught it.

Expected Grade

There appears to be a low positive correlation between student ratings and expected grades. This, of course, could merely reflect the fact that students who expect to receive a relatively high final grade in a course have learned more than those who don't.

Level of the Course

Instructors of higher level courses, especially graduate courses, tend to receive a little higher ratings than those of lower division undergraduate ones. Upper-division undergraduate courses and graduate courses are more likely than lower-division undergraduate ones to be in students' majors and, consequently, they are ones in which students tend to be highly motivated to learn. The higher ratings given to the instructors of such courses, therefore, do not necessarily indicate that the ratings are biased.

Academic Field

Instructors in some fields tend to receive higher teaching ratings than those in others. Those of humanities and arts type courses tend to receive higher ones than those of math-science type courses. Whether these differences reflect deficits in teaching adequacy, student competency, or both is uncertain.

Workload and Difficulty

Contrary to faculty belief, students have a little tendency to give higher ratings to instructors of difficult courses in which it is necessary for them to work hard to learn. Perhaps they do so because they feel good about having been successful in meeting a challenge and/or learning more than they thought they were capable of learning.

Faculty Rank

Regular faculty tend to receive higher teaching ratings than do graduate teaching assistants. This is not particularly surprising since regular faculty usually have more teaching experience, greater knowledge of the subject matter, and more time to invest in preparation than do teaching assistants.

Instructor's Style of Presentation

Instructors who succeed in making their classes both interesting and informative tend to receive higher teaching ratings than those who just succeed in making them informative. This is not particularly surprising since students tend to become more immersed emotionally and intellectually (and consequently learn more) in courses that they regard as being interesting than they do in ones that they regard as being boring.

Whether Rating Sheets Are Signed

Signed ratings tend to be higher than unsigned ones. It's recommended, therefore, that rating sheets not be signed. The reason for signed ratings being higher most likely is that students fear reprisals from the instructors they're rating.

Whether the Instructor Is Present While Students Do the Rating Task

Ratings tend to be higher when the instructor is present, probably for the same reason that they tend to be higher when they aren't anonymous. It is recommended, therefore, that the instructor not be present while the rating sheets are being completed and collected.

Student Knowledge of the Purpose of the Ratings

If the instructions state that the ratings could be used for personnel decisions, they are likely to be higher than if the instructions state that they will be used only by the instructor for improvement. Students tend to be lenient if they believe that their comments and ratings are going to be seen and/or used by persons other than the instructor (assuming, of course, that they like the instructor). It's recommended, therefore, that the purpose(s) for which the ratings will be used be included in the instructions.

Variables That Appear to Have Little or No Impact on Student Ratings of Teaching

Age and Years of Teaching Experience of the Instructor

The studies that have looked at the influence of these variables on student ratings of teaching have detected little or no impact on them. About the only one I'm aware of is older instructors getting slightly lower ratings than younger ones. Whether this deficit is caused by age bias or older instructors not being able to communicate with and/or motivate students as well as younger ones is uncertain. Regardless, the impacts of these variables on student ratings are likely to be too weak to significantly influence judgments of teaching adequacy.

Gender of the Instructor

The findings here are not as clear-cut as they are for most other variables. While there's no compelling evidence that gender is likely to impact significantly on judgments of teaching adequacy, the findings are mixed as to whether a gender-related bias, if it does exist, is likely to favor men or women. Both biases have been reported. A tendency has also been reported for female students to give a little higher ratings to female instructors than to male ones and vice versa.

Race of the Instructor

If an instructor is a member of a minority group, there may be a tendency for students of the same group to rate that instructor a little higher than they would otherwise. However, such a tendency, if it does exist, is unlikely to be strong enough to significantly affect judgments of teaching adequacy.

Personality Traits of the Instructor

Only two personality traits have been shown to significantly affect student ratings. These are *positive self-esteem* and *energy and enthusiasm*. An instructor who has these traits is likely to be a more effective teacher than one who lacks them.

Research Productivity of the Instructor

The correlation between research productivity and student ratings appears to be close to zero. Consequently, an instructor's reputation as a scholar doesn't appear to affect how students view him or her as a teacher. Whether the reason for this low correlation is that being a scholar doesn't make one a better teacher or that students aren't usually aware of their instructor's research productivity is uncertain.

Age of the Student

The correlation between students' ages and their ratings appears to be close to zero.

Gender of the Student

The only effect that has been noted, to the best of my knowledge, is a slight tendency for female students to rate female professors higher than male ones and for male students to rate male professors higher than female ones.

Level of the Student

A slight tendency has been noted for graduate students to give higher ratings than lower-division undergraduate ones. This may merely reflect the fact that the courses graduate students take are almost all in their major and students tend to be more highly motivated to do well in such courses (and consequently learn more) than they are in ones that aren't in their major.

Student's GPA

The correlation between students' GPAs and their ratings appears to be close to zero.

Student's Personality

No student personality traits have been identified, to the best of my knowledge, that appear to significantly affect ratings of teaching.

Class Size

There is a slight tendency for student ratings of teaching to be higher in relatively small classes than in relatively large ones. This tendency may be due, at least in part, to the fact that relatively small classes are more likely to be in the major than are relatively large ones and students tend to be more highly motivated to do well in classes in their major than in others. And, of course, the more motivated they are to do well in a class, the more they are likely to learn.

Time of Day When a Course Is Taught

This variable doesn't usually influence student ratings of teaching significantly. It could do so, however, if a course was taught at a time when students didn't want to be in class, such as at 7:00 A.M. during the week or on a Saturday morning.

Time During the Term When Ratings Are Collected

Any time during the second half of the term appears to yield similar ratings. Apparently, students' opinions about how well a course is being taught tend to be formed by the time the course is half over.

STRATEGIES FOR COPING SUCCESSFULLY WITH STUDENT RATINGS OF TEACHING

Surviving Rating-Related Grieving

It is likely that you'll receive some feedback about the ratings that students gave your teaching. For each course, it may be limited to the average of the average ratings for each of the items on the form, along with that for your department and/or your college or university as a whole. It may also include the average of the ratings for the individual items on the form and/or the forms themselves.

If you are conscientious about teaching, you are likely to find such feedback depressing, at least occasionally. The reason is that you've sustained an injury to your self-concept as a teacher. Whenever people sustain an injury or other kind of loss, they experience the grieving process. It begins with shock and denial, progresses to depression and anger, and then, hopefully, ends with acceptance and the will to get on with life.

I've been a college teacher for more than 30 years, have received a teaching award from my university, but still occasionally get horrible teaching ratings from students. I'm usually able to work my way through the grieving process in about 24 hours. I very much dislike having to grieve for this reason, but accept the need to do so occasionally as an unpleasant but unavoidable part of the job.

Maximizing Ratings for Specific Items

Similar types of items tend to appear on almost all student rating forms for teaching. My main focus for the remainder of this book will be on these items. Specifically, I'll be suggesting strategies based on my experience, my reading, and on structured interviews with college teachers and students for maximizing your ratings on them. Utilizing these strategies is admittedly self-serving. Nevertheless, by doing so you'll be likely to become a more effective teacher.

HOW MEANINGFUL ARE STUDENT RATINGS FOR JUDGING TEACHING?

During most of my career, I've been required to have students rate my teaching at the end of each course. And like most college teachers, I've questioned the validity and reliability of such ratings, particularly when the ones I received were lower than what I expected. At such times, I tended to attribute this to a lack of ability of my students to recognize good teaching.

When I began a search of the literature on student ratings of teaching for this book, I expected to find that whatever research there had been done on them to be equivocal with regard to their validity and reliability. This is not what I found. There have been hundreds of studies that have looked directly or indirectly at the validity and reliability of student ratings of teaching. The findings of almost all of them indicate that both are usually satisfactory, particularly for two category judgments of teaching quality (i.e., adequate or inadequate).

I wish that I had become acquainted with this literature earlier in my teaching career. Perhaps, if I had done so, I would have been more likely to have engaged in some real soul searching when I received lower than expected ratings.

4

Communicating Course Goals, Aims, and Requirements Clearly

All student rating forms for teaching contain an item that requires students to make a judgment about how clearly course goals, aims, and requirements were communicated. If you don't communicate these clearly to your students at the beginning of a course, a number of scenarios can result that are likely to adversely affect (at least a little) the ratings that they give you for this item and possibly, also, what they learn and your job security. The following are a few such scenarios:

- Students claim that they didn't do well on an exam because they didn't know (or didn't know soon enough in advance) that there would be one that day.
- Students claim that they didn't do well on an exam because it wasn't made clear to them what kind of an exam it would be and/or what material would be covered.
- Students claim that they didn't get an assignment in on time because it wasn't clear to them when it was due.
- Students claim that they weren't aware that their grade would be lowered in they had more than a certain number of absences.
- Students fail to understand a course's aims and goals and, consequently, are less likely to study appropriately to achieve them.
- Students sue your college or university because their attorneys claim your syllabus is a contract that you breached and by doing so harmed them (e.g., by giving them a lower grade than the one they deserved).

The traditional way to communicate course goals, aims and requirements is through a printed syllabus that is distributed to students at the beginning of a course. Our focus in this chapter will be on both the makeup and meanings of syllabi to students and others and on strategies for structuring and presenting them so as to communicate course goals, aims, and requirements sufficiently clearly to students that you'll be likely to receive high ratings from them for this aspect of your teaching.

SYLLABI AS LEGAL CONTRACTS

Contractual relationships that will be enforced by the courts are established in ways other than formally signing a document that is labeled a contract or agreement. When you place an order with a waiter or waitress in a restaurant, for example, you assume a contractual obligation to pay for the food you ordered that will be enforced by a court even though you didn't sign anything.

For a relationship to be recognized by the courts as being a contractual one, an offer has to be made and accepted and consideration has to be exchanged. Consideration being exchanged means that each party to the contract agrees to give the other something of value to them. When I accept an offer to purchase a car, for example, the exchange of consideration consists of the dealer giving me the car and my giving the dealer money.

Giving a syllabus to a student at the beginning of a course is highly likely to satisfy the legal requirements for making an offer. And the student attending classes after receiving the syllabus is highly likely to satisfy the legal requirements for accepting an offer. The exchange of consideration here would be the student paying tuition for the course and the instructor (and institution) allowing the student to participate in it and receive credit for doing so.

A syllabus viewed as a contract specifies the obligations of each party to the other. It is necessary for the language in a syllabus, like that in any contract, to specify the obligations of both parties as clearly, unambiguously, and realistically as possible. With regard to the latter, it is crucial that the acquisition of specific knowledge and skills not be promised unless it can be documented that a "reasonable person" (used here as a legal term) would consider the course to be almost certain to provide them. Failing to do so could be viewed by a court as constituting a breach of contract.

Few students and/or their families are likely to threaten a college or university with litigation because they claim a course syllabus is a contract that has been breached by an agent (used here as a legal term) of the institution. Perhaps they would be most likely to do so if a very low grade in a course could prevent a student from graduating or from being licensed or admitted to a graduate school. The clearer and the more realistic the statements of goals, aims, and requirements in your syllabi, the less likely you are to have to undergo the trauma sometime during your academic career of having to assist your institution to defend itself against such a suit or to deal with the threat of one.

SYLLABI AS ROAD MAPS FOR STUDENTS

A syllabus serves as a road map for navigating one's way through a course. Like all such maps, it indicates what it is necessary to do to reach a destination, which in this case is successfully completing the course. And also like all such maps, not consulting it can impede your ability to reach your destination.

Students are likely to consult a syllabus while navigating their way through a course for some or all of the following reasons:

- Information about the instructor, including how and when he or she can be contacted for help.
- Information about the TAs (assuming that there are TAs), including how and when they can be contacted for help.
- A list of required and recommended books and materials.
- A list of readings and where to get them.
- Information about course goals, objectives, and/or concerns.
- An overview of course content.
- A class schedule.
- Information about examinations and other course requirements.
- To find out how much weight the instructor gives to each examination and project when computing final grades.
- The instructor's policies concerning absences, makeup examinations, plagiarism, and other matters.
- Suggestions (hints) for meeting course goals and objectives.

There could also be other reasons for their doing so. If, for example, a syllabus was posted on a website, there could be links on it to sites that contain required or recommended readings.

SYLLABI AS SHIELDS FOR INSTRUCTORS

Syllabi can benefit instructors, as well as students. Perhaps the main way that they are likely to do so is to shield them when "attacked" by students. If course syllabi are both clear (unambiguous) and comprehensive, they can provide a defense against a number of common complaints by students, including those mentioned earlier in this chapter.

SYLLABI AS DOCUMENTATION FOR TENURE
APPLICATIONS

Some departments include course syllabi in applications for tenure or in teaching portfolios (see Chapter 18) that are distributed with tenure applications. Promotion and tenure committees are particularly likely to scrutinize them if student ratings imply that course goals, aims, and requirements aren't being communicated clearly.

ESSENTIAL INFORMATION TO INCLUDE IN A SYLLABUS

There are certain kinds of information that are essential to include in course syllabi if they are to provide both an adequate road map for students and a shield for yourself as well as to cause students and promotion and tenure committee members to conclude that course goals, aims, and requirements were communicated clearly. These are spelled out below.

Basic Information About Yourself and the Course

Information about yourself that you should always include in course syllabi are your full name, office location and/or mailing address, office telephone number, office fax number, e-mail address, and office hours. You should also include your home telephone number if you want students to have the option of contacting you at home. If you do so, you'd be wise to indicate the hours between which it is acceptable for them to call you. You may, also, want to include the address of your personal website if you have one.

Basic information about the course that should be included are the name of the institution, course title and number, semester and year, the location of the class room, credit hours, and meeting times.

Information About the Teaching Assistants (TAs)

If there are TAs, their full names as well as their office locations, office telephone numbers, office fax numbers, e-mail addresses, and office hours, should be included.

Required and Recommended Books and Materials

A list of books and/or materials that students are expected to purchase should be provided. If there are books and/or materials that you recommend but don't require students to purchase, a list of them should be provided also. Furthermore, you may want to indicate where the books and materials can be purchased. If you won't get yourself into trouble with your institution's bookstore for doing so, you may want to list addresses of websites from which required texts can be purchased at a discount. Students are likely to regard your doing so as evidence that you are genuinely interested in them, which could cause the ratings they give you to be a little higher than they would be otherwise.

Reading List(s)

A list of required readings in books, journals, and other publications (including self-published ones) should be provided. If they have been placed "on reserve" and there is more than one campus library, you should indicate which one they're at and the number of hours for which they can be checked out. You may also want to specify the number of copies of each that you have placed "on reserve." Your doing so could discourage students in large classes from delaying reading them until a few days before the examination.

If you are including a session-by-session class schedule, you may want to include with each session a listing of the readings that are relevant to it (instead of having a single reading list for the entire course). If you do this, you may also want to include with each session the pages in the required text(s) that are relevant to topics that will be dealt with during it.

Course Goals, Objectives, and/or Concerns

It should be made clear to students how they are likely to benefit from taking the course. While it may be obvious to you, it may not be obvious to them. And if the course is part of their major or a minor, it should be spelled out how the information presented in it should enhance their understanding of and/or competence to function as a practitioner in their major or minor. It is particularly important to do this for required courses in practitioner-training majors for which the practical implications aren't obvious (e.g., statistics or basic science courses).

Class Schedule

Some instructors include a session-by-session class schedule in their syllabi. That is, they indicate the topic that will be dealt with at each class meeting. There can be both benefits and losses from doing this. If you have taught a course a number of times and can estimate fairly accurately how long you take to cover a particular topic, then the inclusion of such a schedule can be helpful to students as well as convey the message to them that you've given considerable thought to the course. If, however, you include a course schedule and are unable to stick to it because you are unable to estimate accurately how long you take to cover particular topics, its inclusion can lead to confusion and suggest to students that the course wasn't well designed.

Examinations and Other Course Requirements

It is crucial that the dates of the examinations and the material that will be covered on each be communicated clearly. It is also crucial that the types of questions (essay, multiple choice, true or false, fill-in-the-blank, etc.) on them be indicated along with any specific requirements that you have about how they must be answered (e.g., technical terms in answers to fill-in-the-blank questions must be spelled correctly to receive credit).

If you grade on a curve, you should indicate this. Also, you should state your policies regarding make-up examinations for both ones that are missed and ones on which students receive low grades.

Both required papers and projects and extra-credit ones must be described clearly and your expectations for them (e.g., numbers of words) indicated. The date when each is due should, of course, be specified.

Computation of Final Grades

A clear statement here can enable you to avoid many (perhaps most) grade challenges by students. Such a statement should specify the weight given to each examination and project when determining the final course grade. In addition, it should clearly (unambiguously) detail policy violations that can reduce a final course grade, such as unexcused absences and failure to get assignments in on time. Furthermore, it should indicate whether there are extra-credit assignments and if there are, specifically how each affects the final grade. If you don't have extra-credit assignments and fail to indicate this in your syllabi, you're likely to experience the discomfort of having to say "no" to students who beg for them because of low test grades. Such students, incidentally, are likely to give you lower teaching ratings than they would otherwise in order to get even.

Policies Concerning Absences, Makeup Examinations, Plagiarism, and Other Matters

Your policies concerning absences, makeup examinations, plagiarism, and other such course-related matters should be stated as unambiguously as possible. Students who are hurt by one of them are likely to claim that they weren't told about it. Your best defense against such an allegation is to include a clear statement of each such policy in your course syllabi.

SYLLABI ENHANCEMENTS

The items mentioned in the preceding section are ones that should be dealt with routinely in course syllabi. There are others that can enhance their usefulness to students. Several are described here.

Suggestions (Hints) for Meeting Course Goals and Objectives

If your goal is to have as many of your students as possible be successful in meeting course goals and objectives, you may want to include hints for doing so in your syllabi. Their inclusion can be particularly helpful to students who don't know how to begin to achieve a particular goal or objective or who doubt their ability to do so. You could, for example, give some hints for preparing for your type of examination.

Recommended Reading List

You may want to include a bibliography of recommended readings. The inclusion of such a bibliography can both encourage and facilitate students exploring topics dealt with in the course in greater depth and/or from a greater number of perspectives. Annotating such a bibliography is likely to increase its usefulness to students.

Description of In-Class Instructional Format

It may be useful to provide a brief description of your in-class instructional format, particularly if it isn't totally lecture. If students are expected to contribute to class discussions, for example, this could be indicated. Your doing so may motivate them to prepare more adequately for classes— both psychologically and materially—than they would otherwise.

THE WEBSITE OPTION

Some instructors who have a home page on the World Wide Web place their course syllabi on it instead of, or in addition to, distributing it in printed form. While such a syllabus may contain no more information than a printed one, it has the potential to include considerably more information. It can, for example, have links to lecture notes and readings that were authored by the instructor that would be too expensive to distribute in printed form. It can also have links to other websites that contain information relevant to the course. Such information may be communicated by photographs, drawings, audio recordings, and/or video recordings, in addition to by printed words.

STRATEGIES FOR INCREASING AWARENESS OF SYLLABI CONTENT

It isn't safe to assume that distributing a course syllabus in printed form and/or making one available on a website will result in it being read thoughtfully in its entirety. The likelihood of students being aware of its content can be increased significantly by going over it during the first class meeting. Another strategy that can motivate students to read a syllabus thoughtfully in its entirety is to require them to sign a form stating that they have done so. Since few, if any, other instructors at your institution are likely to ask students to sign such a form, the reason for your doing so should be explained to them in a way that doesn't make you appear to be "mean spirited." If you either don't explain it or explain it in a way that appears to be totally self-serving, some students may rate you a little lower than they would otherwise.

5

Creating an Image of Being Knowledgeable About the Subject

All course rating forms contain an item for determining the degree to which the instructor is perceived as being knowledgeable about the subject (field) dealt with in it by his or her students. To receive high ratings for this item, instructors must be both knowledgeable about the content of the courses they teach and communicate their being so to students. Some strategies are described in this chapter that can facilitate your achieving both objectives.

THE NEED TO BE KNOWLEDGEABLE

The need to be knowledgeable is considered here for both courses that are and are not in one's area of expertise. The two are considered separately because the relevant issues are somewhat different.

Courses That Are in Your Areas of Expertise

You will, of course, be expected to be highly knowledgeable about the content of the courses you teach that deal largely with your areas of expertise. Your failure to be so can cause your colleagues to question your competence as a scholar as well as a teacher. Someone who doesn't understand a field well is unlikely to be able to formulate research questions that are sufficiently original and meaningful to either earn him or her a strong national reputation as a scholar or be the recipient of substantial extramural funding. Both are requirements for tenure in some departments.

Courses That Are Not in Your Areas of Expertise

Ideally, all of the courses you'll be expected to teach will be ones about which you are highly knowledgeable. The reality, however, is that you'll probably be expected to teach at least one course in which there is a great deal of subject matter about which you are not highly knowledgeable. Few departments have faculty who are highly knowledgeable about the content of every course they offer.

Junior faculty, particularly new hires, are more likely than senior ones to be assigned courses to teach for which both they and the other faculty in their department lack expertise. There are at least two reasons. First, the choice of courses to teach in most departments is based on seniority and they are "low man on the totem pole." Most (perhaps all) of the senior faculty in their department probably will want to continue teaching the courses they've been teaching, particularly if the courses deal largely with topics in which they have both interest and expertise. An additional benefit that they may derive from teaching courses they've taught previously is having to spend little time on preparation.

A second reason why a junior faculty member may be assigned to teach such a course is the hope that he or she will both develop an interest in and become knowledgeable about that subject matter. If this were to happen, there would be one less course the department offers that is taught by an instructor who lacks interest and expertise in its content.

What usually happens when instructors are assigned to teach courses in which they have little interest or expertise is for them to use the textbook as the main (perhaps the only) source for organization and content. They present little, or no, information that clearly goes beyond that in the textbook. Consequently, their students don't tend to view them as knowledgeable about what they teach and will rate them accordingly.

You can "go along with the herd" and invest little of yourself when assigned to teach such courses. And your likelihood of being tenured probably won't be reduced significantly by doing so (assuming, of course, that you are adequately knowledgeable about the content of the courses you teach in your areas of expertise). There are some reasons, however, why you may choose to not go along with the herd—that is, choose to become knowledgeable about the subject matter dealt with in them—including the following:

- To increase your teaching ratings.
- To make teaching them more enjoyable.
- To increase your possibilities for developing a national reputation as a scholar and for securing extramural funding.
- To make you less likely to experience "burnout."

Some implications of each are dealt with here.

To Increase Your Teaching Ratings

If you are knowledgeable about the subject matter in a course, students are likely to give you higher overall teacher ratings than they are otherwise. They are unlikely to give a course a high overall rating if they don't consider the instructor to be knowledgeable about its content (unless the instructor at the beginning of the course frankly acknowledged not to be knowledgeable about it and successfully challenged the students to become so along with him or her).

To Make Teaching Them More Enjoyable

Few instructors are likely to find teaching a course enjoyable when they know that their understanding of its content is veneer thin and their students do also. Even if your institution gives little weight to teaching when making tenure decisions, it's still worthwhile to become sufficiently knowledgeable about the content of the courses you teach that lie outside your areas of expertise to teach them well, if for no other reason than maintaining your mental health. Few instructors can avoid becoming depressed after receiving low teaching ratings, even if they're for assigned courses about which they care little.

To Increase Your Possibilities for Developing a National Reputation as a Scholar and for Securing Extramural Funding

Few professors are likely to invest in becoming knowledgeable about a field in which they didn't specialize in graduate school if they aren't "strongly encouraged" (i.e., forced) to do so. Such a scenario would be being assigned to teach a course that either lies outside their field or deals with an aspect of it in which they have little or no expertise. While acquiring the information needed to teach the course, they're likely to become aware of topics or questions for research that they're unlikely to have otherwise. These could be ones that, if pursued, would be more likely to yield a national reputation as a scholar and/or extramural grant funding than those they're currently pursuing. Acquiring such information, at the very least, would increase their options for pursuing both.

To Make You Less Likely to Experience "Burnout"

I've taught at the college level for more than 30 years. If I'd been teaching the same courses once or twice every academic year throughout this period, it's highly likely that by now I wouldn't have found doing so intellectually challenging and would have experienced "burnout." A strategy that I've used throughout my academic career to keep myself from experiencing burnout is volunteering to teach courses in emerging areas about which my knowledge, if I had any, was veneer thin before preparing to teach them. Doing so, incidentally, has yielded (directly or indirectly) more than six books and 75 journal articles.

BECOMING KNOWLEDGEABLE

There are a number of ways you can learn about a field that your knowledge of is veneer thin. The ones I've used include the following:

• Reading books, journals, newsletters, and copies of convention and conference presentations.
• Searching and otherwise utilizing the Internet.
• Taking workshops and attending relevant sessions at professional meetings.
• Acquiring a "mentor."
• Pursuing training during a sabbatical.

Each of these is commented on below.

Reading Books, Journals, Newsletters, and Copies of Convention and Conference Presentations

These are the main ways I've gotten information about fields, or parts of fields, that I knew little or nothing about. For emerging fields, newsletter articles and copies of convention and conference presentations tend to be more useful than books and articles in peer-reviewed journals. The reason is that the information in them is more likely to be at the "cutting edge" of knowledge in a field because the delay between acceptance and publication tends to be shorter than for articles in peer-reviewed journals and books. A delay of a year or more isn't unusual after a manuscript has been accepted for publication by a book publisher or the editor of a peer-reviewed journal. Information from newsletters and convention and conference presentations has to be scrutinized more carefully than that from peer-reviewed journal articles and books, because the former are unlikely to have been subjected to a rigorous peer-review process before being accepted for publication.

Searching and Otherwise Utilizing the Internet

The World Wide Web has become the first source I utilize when seeking information about a topic, particularly one in an emerging field. I utilize a search engine for doing so. It sometimes takes a few tries to locate the information I'm seeking because the key words I use initially aren't the appropriate ones. The websites I identify through such a search usually include at least one that contains a listing of relevant journal articles and books. Since the information on most websites was not subjected to a peer-review process before being posted, its validity and reliability is less certain than that in articles in peer-reviewed journals and books.

Another possible source of information on the Internet is listservs and news groups. These exist for most fields. They are particularly useful for getting answers to specific questions. You could, for example, request information about sources (books, journal articles, etc.) for particular kinds of information. You may even want to set up a listserv (assuming that one doesn't already exist) that would enable you to share information about what works and what doesn't with some of those who teach a particular course and they with you.

Still another possible source of information on the Internet is articles in electronic journals. Some such journals subject submitted papers to a rigorous peer-review process and others do not. The information in electronic journals is likely to be more up-to-date than that in print journals because the publication delay tends to be shorter.

E-mail is perhaps the most useful tool for obtaining information from the Internet. You could, for example, use it to get some help from instructors at other institutions who teach a course you are either preparing to teach or want to teach more effectively. Most such instructors, particularly ones who take real pride in their teaching, probably would be willing to provide such help (assuming, of course, that the amount of help you are requesting is reasonable).

Taking Workshops and Attending Relevant Sessions at Professional Meetings

Doing both can be very helpful, particularly when you're beginning to acquaint yourself with a field.

Acquiring a "Mentor"

It may be possible to find someone who teaches a course you are preparing to teach or want to each more effectively who will serve as a "mentor." Ideally, this should be someone who teaches the course well. Most instructors would be flattered to be asked.

Pursuing Training During a Sabbatical

An acceptable activity for a sabbatical at most institutions is preparing to teach a new course or an existing one more effectively. It could involve doing a post-doctoral at another institution.

COMMUNICATING BEING KNOWLEDGEABLE TO STUDENTS

To get a high rating for this, you not only have to knowledgeable about what you teach but communicate your being so to students. There are a number of do's and don'ts for doing so, including the following:

- Don't give students the impression that the reason you're teaching the course is that none of the other faculty in your department wanted to teach it.
- Present information that isn't in the textbook.
- Refer to "authorities" in the field other than the author of the textbook you're using.
- Present concepts to students in ways that are meaningful to them.
- Present well-thought-through opinions about controversial subjects.
- Encourage students to express points-of-view that differ from yours.
- Encourage students to ask questions and answer them in a way that indicates your knowledge isn't veneer thin.
- If you don't know the answer to a question, admit it.
- Talk "to" not "at" your students.
- Convey a genuine interest in and enthusiasm for the field.
- Share your research in the field with students.
- Make students aware of your reputation in the field—assuming, of course, that you have already established a regional, national, or international one.

Some strategies for accomplishing each of these are suggested below.

Don't Give Students the Impression That the Reason You're Teaching the Course Is That None of the Other Faculty in Your Department Wanted to Teach It

I can recall several occasions while I was a student when an instructor communicated at the beginning of a course that he or she was teaching it because of having been assigned to do so. While such honesty may be commendable, it is unlikely to yield high ratings for being knowledgeable because it is likely to alter students' assumptions regarding how knowledgeable the instructor is. Students usually tend to assume that instructors are knowledgeable about the content of the courses they teach. However, when an instructor tells them that he or she is teaching a course because it has to be taught and nobody else in the department wants to teach it, they're less likely than otherwise to view the professor as being knowledgeable about it's content. And if they have a set to view an instructor as not being knowledgeable, they're likely to have little difficulty finding evidence to support their belief.

Present Information That Isn't in the Textbook

Instructors who limit their lectures and responses to students' questions to information in the textbook are unlikely to be considered highly knowledgeable by their students. Consequently, it's a good idea to present at least a little information from sources other than the textbook, such as:

- Books intended for professionals and scholars.
- Journal articles that were published after the textbook was published.
- Convention/conference presentations.
- The World Wide Web.
- Internet listservs and news groups.
- Letters and e-mail messages.
- Personal experience.

There, of course, could be other such sources.

Refer to "Authorities" in the Field Other than the Author of the Textbook You're Using

It can be helpful if you're acquainted with (or better yet, were trained by) persons who are regarded as authorities in the field to make your students aware of it. However, remember that such "name dropping" is likely to turn students off if overdone.

Present Concepts to Students in Ways That Are Meaningful to Them

You have to understand a concept well to communicate it clearly to students. Consequently, students tend to assume that instructors who are able to explain difficult concepts in ways they can understand are knowledgeable about what they're teaching.

Present Well Thought-Through Opinions About Controversial Subjects

You have to be knowledgeable about a controversial subject to be able to offer a well thought-through (cogent) opinion about it. This fact tends to be understood by students. Consequently, a way to communicate to students that you're knowledgeable about what you're teaching is to offer such an opinion whenever it seems appropriate to do so.

Encourage Students to Express Points of View That Differ from Yours

Persons who aren't knowledgeable about the subject matter they're teaching are unlikely to encourage students to express points of view that differ from theirs. Consequently, an instructor who encourages students to express such points of view is likely to be regarded by them as being highly knowledgeable.

Encourage Students to Ask Questions and Answer Them in a Way That Indicates Your Knowledge Isn't Veneer Thin

Persons who aren't highly knowledgeable about what they're teaching rarely encourage students to ask questions that go beyond what's in the textbook. And when they answer students' questions, they tend to do so at a depth that suggest they aren't very knowledgeable and/or experienced. Consequently, one way to communicate to students that you're knowledgeable about a subject is to encourage them to ask questions about it that requires information that isn't in the textbook.

If You Don't Know the Answer to a Question, Admit It

Persons who are insecure regarding their knowledge of what they're teaching tend to be more likely than those who aren't to answer questions to which they don't really know the answer. And their answers are likely to reveal their lack of knowledge by being superficial and/or inaccurate.

Incidentally, persons who are highly motivated to teach well tend to welcome being asked relevant questions to which they don't know the answer. There are at least two reasons. First, such questions suggest concepts or topics about which they need to acquire information and/or formulate opinions. And second, they provide an opportunity to model for students the appropriate way to react when you don't know the answer to a question.

Talk "to" Not "at" Your Students

If you are knowledgeable about what you're teaching, but you communicate poorly, they're likely to rate you as being less knowledgeable than you really are. Keeping them awake requires you to talk *to* them rather than *at* them. That is, it requires you to be an effective communicator.

Convey a Genuine Interest in and Enthusiasm for the Field

Instructors are more likely to evince a genuine interest in and enthusiasm for the contents of courses about which they are knowledgeable than they are for the contents of those about which they aren't. Consequently, students are likely to equate an instructor evincing a high level of interest in and enthusiasm for a course with that instructor being knowledgeable about its content if both the interest and enthusiasm appear to be genuine.

Share Your Research in the Field with Students

Persons who publish in a field are likely to be regarded by students as being knowledgeable about it. Consequently, one way to communicate that you're knowledgeable about what you're teaching is by making students aware of a few of your contributions to the literature of the field(s) with which your courses deal. It's crucial, however, that this be done in a way that doesn't make you appear to be "patting yourself on the back" and/or devoting considerable class time to particular topics or issues merely because they're ones on which your research and writings have focused. Either can result in you receiving lower teaching ratings than you probably would have otherwise.

Make Students Aware of Your Reputation in the Field— Assuming, of Course, That You Have Already Established a Regional, National, or International One

Persons who have a regional, national, or international reputation in a field tend to be regarded as being knowledgeable about it. If you have such a reputation, you'd be wise to make your students aware of it. However, they may interpret your doing it as "patting yourself on the back." Consequently, it would be best to have someone else do it, possibly a guest speaker.

6

Enhancing Students' Motivation

Motivation is crucial to learning. Both what students learn in a course and the length of time they retain it are affected by their instructor's ability to enhance their motivation. And their instructor's ability to do so can profoundly affect the teaching ratings that they give to him or her. A number of factors that can affect an instructor's ability to enhance his or her students' motivation are dealt with in this chapter.

MOTIVATION—A PREREQUISITE FOR INVESTING TO LEARN

To learn you must invest. The investment necessary to acquire particular knowledge could include time, money, energy, the willingness to be uncomfortable, and/or some or all of these. Since the amount of each that you have to invest is finite, a decision to invest them to acquire particular knowledge means that you'll have less of them to invest to acquire other knowledge.

Your willingness to invest to achieve a particular goal is determined, in large part, by the benefits you expect to receive from achieving it. Your expectations may or may not be realistic. Regardless, if you expect the benefits you'll be receiving to be substantial, you're more likely to invest than if you don't.

One way to gauge the amount you'd expect to benefit from achieving a particular goal is to answer the following hypothetical questions: If I were to achieve this goal, in what specific ways would my life be likely to be affected? What would I begin doing that I don't do now? What would I cease doing (that I don't like doing) that I do now? What positive impacts would it have on both my work (professional) and social lives? In what ways, if any, could I be worse off by achieving it than I am now? If your answers to these questions suggest that the benefits you'd expect to receive from achieving the goal far outweigh the potential losses, you'd be likely to make the necessary investments. If, on the other hand, your answers indicate that achieving the goal would be likely to have little or no positive impact on your life, you'd be unlikely to make the investments that would have to be made to achieve it.

The investments that students have to be willing to make to be successful academically are likely to be substantial. Consequently, it is necessary that they be highly motivated to succeed in this way if they are to make them. This is particularly likely to be true if there are other goals they'd like to achieve while in college that require some or all of the same investments (e.g., having a decent social life or finding a spouse).

WHAT DO WE WANT TO ENHANCE OUR STUDENTS' MOTIVATION TO DO?

An instructor who doesn't attempt to enhance students' motivation to benefit from taking his or her courses is unlikely to be tenured. A student may benefit from taking a course in one or more of the following ways:

- Meet a requirement for graduation.
- Maintain or increase his or her overall GPA.
- Please someone.
- Learn something new.
- Acquire knowledge and/or skills.
- Learn how to acquire knowledge and/or improve skills independently.
- Enjoy!

Each is discussed below.

Meet a Requirement for Graduation

If a student is motivated at all to get something from a course, it's likely to be to fulfill a requirement for graduation. The requirement could be the course itself and/or the credits earned by passing it. Most questions that are asked in class by students who have this as their primary goal are likely to pertain to the content and format of the examinations. Such a question would be "Are we going to be tested on ——— ?" I've frequently gotten this question prior to audio-visual presentations and outside speakers. A student who asks mostly this type of question is unlikely to pay much attention to material on which he or she isn't going to be tested. Furthermore, he or she is unlikely to be highly motivated to learn course material sufficiently well to retain it after being tested. It, of course, isn't necessary to do so to achieve this goal.

Maintain or Increase His or Her Overall GPA

A student may be motivated to earn a good grade in a course to get or keep his or her overall GPA high enough to do one or more of the following:

- Graduate.
- Be eligible to participate in an activity (e.g., a sport such as football).
- Be admitted to graduate school.
- Receive financial aid.
- Receive academic honors.

To achieve any of these goals, it isn't necessary to learn course material well enough to retain it after being tested.

Please Someone

A student may be motivated to do well in a course to please a parent or someone else. This could be the instructor, particularly if he or she has a national reputation in the field that the student majors or plans to major. A strong recommendation from such a person could be helpful for getting a job or being admitted to graduate school. To achieve this goal (as was the case for the previous two) it isn't necessary to learn course material well enough to retain it after being tested.

Learn Something New

This goal, unlike the previous three, requires a student to learn course material well enough to retain it after completing the course. While there is a positive relationship between a student's final grade in a course and the amount of material from it that he or she retains a year or more after completing the course, the relationship is far from perfect. Some students learn considerably more about the subject matter of the courses that they take than their final grades in them would suggest. They may, for example, be more strongly motivated to spend their time learning than cramming to get high grades on examinations. Such students, when they become interested in a subject, are likely to spend considerable time exploring it in ways on which they won't necessarily be tested. For them, acquiring knowledge is more important than acquiring grades. Such students, incidentally, are more likely to keep—not sell—their textbooks (particularly ones for courses in their major) than are those who are motivated primarily by one or more of the previous three goals.

Acquire Knowledge and/or Skills

This goal, like the previous one, requires a student to learn course material well enough to retain it after completing the course. And, as I've indicated previously, while there is a positive relationship between a student's final grade in a course and the amount of material from it that he or she retains, the relationship is far from perfect. Students can acquire more knowledge and improve their skills to a greater extent than their grades would indicate. The likelihood of this type of disparity depends, in part, on how students are tested. It would be less likely to happen if examinations required students to apply knowledge and demonstrate skills than it would if they merely required students to memorize material from lectures and/or books and articles and regurgitate it.

Learn How to Acquire Knowledge and/or Improve Skills Independently

Students, to survive, are going to have to acquire knowledge and improve skills throughout their life. It's crucial, therefore, that they learn how to do both independently. That is, it's crucial that they learn the skills that they will need to be able to teach themselves. We can facilitate their learning by enhancing both their motivation to acquire these skills and their confidence in their ability to use them effectively. This should be one of our main goals—perhaps our main goal—as college teachers. And our accepting it as such would have a number of implications both for what we would expect our students to do and how we would interact with them. This conviction is reflected in the points of view presented and the recommendations made throughout the book.

Enjoy!

One benefit that a student may derive from taking a course is a new option for enjoying life. While a course in art or music appreciation can obviously yield such a benefit, so can any other course. The act of learning more about anything can be pleasurable.

EXTRINSIC FORMS OF MOTIVATION ENHANCEMENT

There are two forms of motivation enhancement that an instructor can use: extrinsic and intrinsic. Extrinsic motivators are "carrots" that a professor dangles in front of students to motivate them, such as grades and being liked by him or her. Intrinsic motivators are ones that tend to satisfy basic human needs, such as curiosity, feeling competent, and achieving. The distinction between the two is not always sharp. We will focus in this section on extrinsic forms of motivation enhancement and in the next on intrinsic ones.

Extrinsic forms of motivation enhancement, by themselves, can only help students achieve some of the goals mentioned in the previous section. And their ability to motivate may only be for a relatively short period of time, because if they aren't increased periodically, students are likely to satiate to them. When this happens, they cease being sufficiently meaningful to students to motivate them. Extrinsic forms of motivation enhancement can, however, be very effective as a means to an end, the end being an increased "openness" to various forms of intrinsic motivation enhancement. The pro's and con's of several of the more common forms of extrinsic motivation enhancement are considered below.

Grades

Grades are a powerful motivational tool. Almost all students are motivated to get at least passing grades. Unfortunately, they are more likely to motivate students to do what is necessary to get good grades than to acquire knowledge and/or skills they will retain and use.

While the use of grades as a motivator does have a downside, they can, nevertheless, be useful as a motivational tool. Grades can be used to induce students to get through some of the drudgery of initial learning, thereby making them receptive to various forms of intrinsic motivation enhancement.

Honors, Awards, and Scholarships

While these can be powerful motivational tools, they (like grades) are more likely to motivate students to do what is necessary to get them than to acquire knowledge and/or skills that they will retain and use. However, they (also like grades) can be used to induce students to get through some of the drudgery of initial learning, thereby making them receptive to various forms of intrinsic motivation enhancement.

Pleasing a Parent, a Teacher, or Someone Else

The desire to please, be liked by, and/or be respected by someone can be a powerful motivator. The someone can be a parent (or other family member), a teacher, a friend, a mentor, or some other "authority" figure. What a person believes he or she has to do to please, be liked by, and/or respected by this person determines whether this would be a form of extrinsic or of intrinsic motivation enhancement. If it is to get good grades, or things associated with them such as honors (being on the Dean's List), awards, or scholarships, then this would be a form of extrinsic motivation enhancement. However, if it is to acquire knowledge and/or skills—with grades merely being a byproduct of acquiring them—then this would be a form of intrinsic motivation enhancement.

When used as a tool for extrinsic motivation enhancement, it has the same limitations as grades, honors, awards, and scholarships. However, like these extrinsic motivation enhancers, it can also serve as a means to a desirable end—that is, inducing students to get through some of the drudgery of initial learning, thereby increasing their receptivity to their motivation being enhanced intrinsically.

INTRINSIC FORMS OF MOTIVATION ENHANCEMENT

Our goal as teachers, perhaps our primary goal, should be to motivate students to learn to teach themselves. One way that we can do this is to nurture their curiosity, thereby strengthening their desire to want to learn more. Another is to reinforce the pleasure that they receive (like we all do) from learning to do things well. The reward for learning in both instances would be satisfying an internal need rather than getting something from someone (e.g., grades, awards, or recommendations). A number of ways that teachers can nurture (strengthen) their students' internal need to learn are indicated in this section.

Focusing on Questions Rather than Answers

Questions arouse students' curiosity, but answers usually don't unless they suggest further questions. One characteristic of the scientific method, which some philosophers of science refer to as comprehensiveness or scope of knowledge, is the following:

Instead of presenting a finished account of the world, the genuine scientist keeps his unifying hypotheses open to revision and is always ready to modify or abandon them if evidence should render them doubtful. This *self corrective aspect* [italics mine] of science has rightly been stressed as its most important characteristic. . . . It is a sign of one's maturity to be able to live with an unfinished world view. (Feigl, 1955, p. 13)

Consequently, students would be encouraged to regard all questions as having only tentative answers for which they may be able to provide better or viable alternative ones. Such a belief can be internally motivating for learning because even attempting to meet the challenge of coming up with more accurate and/or complete answers is likely to be pleasurable.

Pleasing Someone

This can function as an intrinsic form of motivation enhancement rather than an extrinsic one. It depends on what a student has to do to please. If, for example, it is to attempt to come up with more accurate and/or complete answers to questions, it could facilitate their learning to motivate and teach themselves and would, therefore, be a form of intrinsic motivation enhancement.

Increasing Awareness of the Need for Learning

Making students aware of the internal need that learning and retaining particular material would satisfy for them is a form of intrinsic motivation enhancement. A frequent mistake that teachers make is assuming that the need for learning certain material is obvious. While it may be obvious to them, it probably isn't to at least some of their students. If it were obvious, their students would be learning it for long-term retention, not "cramming" it a few days before the examination on which it's covered.

Interest

Students are likely to be motivated to learn about things in which their interest has been aroused. Consequently, an instructor can enhance students' motivation to learn particular material by providing them with experiences that cause them to regard it as interesting. Such experiences, for example, could include engaging in role playing and other simulations, providing opportunities to observe and/or participate in relevant activities, and lecturing in ways that are likely to arouse student interest. The latter is particularly important in required courses, particularly ones that aren't a part of a student's major. Most of the students in them are unlikely, at least initially, to be highly interested in the subject matter.

Success in Learning

Nothing succeeds like success nor fails like failure. Students tend to be motivated to learn more about what they have previously experienced success learning and tend to be "turned off" on learning about what they have previously experienced failure in trying to learn. Anything an instructor can do to build students' confidence in their ability to learn is likely to increase their attempts to do so, at least a little. Unfortunately, the opposite is also true. Causing students to question their ability to learn is likely to result in fewer attempts to do so. And the less a student invests in learning, the more likely he or she is to fail. Consequently, the expectation to fail can become a self-fulfilling prophecy.

Try to recall a teacher who impacted on you in ways that significantly changed your life for the better. Perhaps it was the teacher who initially aroused your interest in your field. Was making you feel competent as a learner one of the reasons (perhaps the main one) that teacher impacted on you to the extent he or she did? If your answer is yes, you've experienced the positive impact a teacher can have on a student's motivation to learn.

Now, try to recall some subject matter that you doubt your ability to learn. For many of us, it's math. Were comments and/or actions by a teacher at least partially responsible for your doubting your ability? If your answer is yes, you've experienced the negative impact a teacher can have on a student's motivation to learn.

Perhaps the main way that we, as teachers, can be helpful to our students is to encourage them to feel competent. Some strategies for doing so are presented in the next section.

STRATEGIES FOR ENHANCING A STUDENT'S MOTIVATION TO LEARN

As I've indicated previously, there are a number of ways that teachers can enhance their students' motivation to learn. Some of them are dealt with in this section. The order in which they are dealt with isn't intended to indicate their importance for either motivating students or securing high ratings from them.

Don't Overemphasize Grades or Other Extrinsic Motivators

Most college teachers, including myself, use grades and other extrinsic motivators to get students to prepare for examinations and to do assignments. This is frequently, particularly in large classes, the main way that college teachers attempt to enhance their students' motivation to learn. While they may perform well enough to get good grades and a feeling of accomplishment, their feeling of accomplishment is likely to result from the grades they receive rather than from the acquisition of new knowledge/skills or being better able to acquire them.

Grades and other extrinsic motivators, as I've indicated previously, can be used to promote a feeling of accomplishment from acquiring new knowledge and skills and/or the tools needed to acquire them. To do so, it's necessary for applications of knowledge and skills to be graded rather than merely "regurgitations" of them. While it tends to take more time to do this, the feeling of accomplishment it yields both you and your students is likely to cause you to consider the additional time to be time well spent.

Grade Students in Ways That Are Likely to Make Them Feel Competent

Relatively high grades are more likely than relatively low ones to make students feel competent. And consequently, they are more likely to enhance their motivation to learn more.

During my 30-plus years of college teaching, I've contributed significantly to what has been referred to as "grade inflation," and I don't apologize for doing so. I've used grades for both motivation enhancement and evaluation and, throughout this period, have considered their former function to be more important than their latter. I've set goals for my courses that almost all students, *with effort*, could achieve and if they achieved them, I gave them high grades. My goal (which I, unfortunately, achieved only a few times) was for every student to acquire enough knowledge and/or hone his or her clinical skills sufficiently to earn an "A" as a final grade. As a result, a higher percentage of students leave my courses feeling both good about themselves and competent to learn more than they probably would have otherwise.

Low grades for a knowledge or skill area can cause students to question their competence to perform well in it for the rest of their lives. Many of us were convinced by the grades we received in elementary school that we lack competence in such areas as math, art, music, and athletics. And our having such a belief is likely to discourage us from trying to perform them better or learn more about them, thereby yielding a self-fulfilling prophecy and causing our potential for both enjoyment and achievement to decrease.

Make Students Feel That They Are Valued as People by Learning Their Names and in Other Ways

The more valued a teacher makes a student feel, the more likely the student is to be motivated to learn from the teacher—that is, the more likely that the teacher will become a role model for the student. One way to make a student feel valued is to learn his or her name. A number of other strategies for making students feel valued as people are presented in Chapter 8.

Remove Barriers That Prevent Students from Enjoying Learning

Such barriers result from teachers behaving in ways that reduce their students' motivation to learn, including the following:

- Causing students to feel stupid or embarrassed when they answer a question or perform a task incorrectly.

- Using teaching practices that are ineffective or mismatched to the students' abilities, experience, and/or learning styles.
- Providing infrequent, insincere, or vague feedback about performance (i.e., providing inadequate positive reinforcement).
- Giving assignments for which lack of success is probable or feared.
- Giving assignments that students consider irrelevant—that is, time-consuming "busy work" from which they tend to learn little or nothing.
- Resorting to sarcasm, put-downs, or criticism that causes students to "lose face."

These, of course, are not the only ways that teachers can erect such barriers.

Provide Students with Opportunities for Self-Actualization

You do this for your students by giving them opportunities to set their own goals and motivate themselves to achieve them. Your role becomes that of a consultant (i.e., a resource person). By providing students such opportunities, you're likely to both strengthen their capability to function independently and their confidence in their ability to do so.

Make the Course Appear to Be Relevant by Documenting the Needs That It Satisfies for Students

Students are more likely to be motivated to learn material and acquire skills if they believe that doing so will benefit them in some way now and/ or in the future. Consequently, it is crucial that students believe strongly when they begin a course that they're likely to benefit from learning the material or acquiring the skills that they'll be expected to learn or acquire. While the ways they are likely to benefit may seem obvious to you, it isn't safe to assume that *all* of them will be obvious to *all* of the students. Time spent at the beginning of a course detailing potential benefits is highly likely to be time well spent. While doing so may not affect the motivation of the brightest students, it's likely to enhance that of at least a few of the others.

Make Your Teaching Appropriate for Your Students' Experience, Capacity, and Needs

One of the most frequent errors that instructors, particularly beginning ones, make is teaching in ways that are inappropriate for their students' experience, capacity, and/or needs. And by doing so, they are likely to "turn off" at least a few students.

One of the most frequent errors that instructors make with regard to experience is assuming that students remember what they learned in previous courses. Consequently, they don't review concepts that students must understand if elaborations on them and/or new ones are to be meaningful. Without such a review, at least a few students are likely to feel over- whelmed and, consequently, will tend to invest less in learning course ma- terial than they would have otherwise. While an instructor, with considerable justification, can view this as a failure of his or her students to live up to their responsibilities (i.e., learning material well enough to retain it long-term), the reality is that viewing it this way is likely to sig- nificantly reduce the amount that some students will learn. And it's also likely to result in the instructor receiving lower teaching ratings than he or she would have otherwise.

Another error instructors (particularly beginning ones) may make that can adversely affect their students' motivation is under- or overestimating their capacity to learn. If a course is taught at too low a level, students are unlikely to feel challenged and, consequently, they're unlikely to feel highly motivated to learn. They're also likely to view the instructor as treating them in a condescending manner and/or not respecting them. Consequently, they're likely to give him or her relatively low teaching ratings.

Teaching a course at too high a level can also adversely affect students' motivation to learn. Beginning instructors are, perhaps, more likely to make this error than teaching at too low a level. There are at least two reasons they may do so. First, they may assume that their students have the same capacity to learn that they have. They may forget that all undergraduates aren't capable of learning at the level required for success in graduate school. And second, they may be motivated to impress their students with the size of their vocabulary and/or the depth of their knowledge. Regardless of the reason for doing so, the result is likely to be the same—a failure to communicate resulting in all but the brightest students being less motivated than they would have been otherwise. And as a consequence, the teaching ratings the instructor receives will probably be lower than they would have been otherwise.

An instructor may also make the error of misjudging his or her students' needs by presenting information at a depth or from a perspective that is inappropriate. A speech pathologist, for example, doesn't have to under- stand the anatomy and physiology of the brain in the same way as does a neurosurgeon. An instructor who attempts to present neuroanatomy and physiology to students majoring in speech pathology in the same way that he or she would to medical students is likely to "turn off" many of them.

Teach in Ways That Are Likely to Excite Student Interest and Curiosity

To motivate students, you need to get and hold their attention. Being in a classroom doesn't automatically cause students to attend to and process what the instructor is saying and/or doing. To get them to do both, it's necessary to excite their interest and curiosity. A number of strategies are presented in this section that are likely to increase the odds of doing both.

Exhibit Enthusiasm About the Course

If you seem bored or ambivalent about material you teach, you are less likely to excite your students' interest and curiosity in it and, consequently, they're less likely to be motivated to learn it for long-term retention. On the other hand, if you are enthusiastic about the material and seem to enjoy teaching it, you are likely to both hold their attention and arouse their curiosity. Consequently, you'd be wise on the first day of class to talk enthusiastically about why the material you'll be teaching is likely to be relevant for them now or in the future.

Inject Yourself into the Course

A teacher whom students consider human and accessible is more likely to excite their interest and curiosity than one whom they regard as being merely an information-generating entity. Relating anecdotes about your personal experiences in the field that reinforce what you are teaching is likely to get and hold their attention. So is talking about and otherwise communicating your excitement in teaching the subject and being in the field.

Begin Each Class by Telling Students What You're Going to Tell Them

One widely used formula for organizing an oral presentation consists of three steps: (1) tell them what you're going to tell them, (2) tell them, and (3) tell them what you told them. Beginning each class session by briefly outlining the material you'll be covering that day makes it easier for students to follow it and take notes, thereby increasing the likelihood that they'll both attend to and process the material. It may also facilitate their learning to summarize briefly at the end of each class what you dealt with during it.

Vary Teaching Methods

Most students find it difficult to maintain a high level of attention/concentration for even as short a time as 45 minutes when lecturing is the only teaching method used. One way that an instructor can, at least partially, remedy this situation is to break up long periods of lecturing by doing things such as the following:

- Encouraging students to ask questions whenever they occur to them.
- Giving students frequent short "stand up and walk around" breaks.
- Having discussions about aspects of the material on which you're lecturing that

involve either the entire class or small groups within it (into which you divided the class).

- Role-playing.
- Using films, audiotapes, videotapes, and/or computer multimedia presentations.
- Demonstrating!
- Having guest lecturers.
- Having students do presentations.
- Having field trips.

There, of course, may be other activities you can use that will both break up long periods of lecturing and facilitate achieving course goals.

Tell Stories

Telling stories can help to get and hold students' attention. It can also get them to grasp course concepts. The following comments by a philosophy professor illustrate their value:

I tell a lot of stories. Stories are nails that I hammer into the wall. On those nails I hang up the whole, usually highly abstract, conceptual stuff of a philosophy course. If there are no nails in the wall, all of the stuff falls down and will be forgotten. But if there are stories, illustrations, visualizations, they will not be forgotten, and contained in the stories are the problems and the concepts. Years latter students will remember the stories and because of the stories, still understand the concepts. (Anonymous)

Use Humor

Humor, like telling stories, can get and hold students' attention. It can also help to break down student-teacher barriers to communication. It is less likely than otherwise to be effective for accomplishing these goals if it's self-disparaging, forced, inappropriate, at the expense of students or colleagues, sexist, or bigoted. If you're uncomfortable using humor while teaching, you'd be wise to refrain from doing so because students will sense this and, consequently, your using it will be unlikely to be effective.

Aim for Understanding Rather than Memorization

Understanding a concept is likely to be more motivation-enhancing than memorizing the words pertaining to it. It will, also, both lead to longer retention and make the concept more useful. And because students are likely to feel that they've learned more if they understand the concepts that were taught in a course rather than merely memorizing definitions of them, teaching for understanding will tend to yield higher teaching ratings for the instructor.

Have Expectations for Students That Are as High as They Are Capable of Attaining

One of my professors in graduate school (Dr. Wendell Johnson) was regarded as being a great teacher, in part, because he motivated students to achieve at levels beyond which they thought they were capable of achieving. He understood tacitly the levels at which students were capable of achieving and enhanced their motivation in ways that caused them to either achieve at this level or came closer to doing so than they would have otherwise. Students who are impacted by a teacher in this way will almost always rate his or her teaching very highly.

Clearly State Your Expectations

The amount that students are likely to invest in learning course material is, in part, a function of what they believe they will have to invest to meet their teacher's expectations. Consequently, if you want to motivate your students to perform at a relatively high level, state clearly what they will need to do to perform at this level.

Give Students Frequent, Understandable, and Usable Feedback That's Unlikely to Discourage Them

Letting students know that they're making progress toward achieving a goal will tend to encourage them to continue to work toward achieve it. And giving them feedback in a way that's unlikely to discourage them about how they need to modify what they're doing to achieve a goal will also tend to encourage them to work toward achieving it.

Encourage Students to Connect Success (or Failure) with the Amount of Effort Expended

Thomas Edison was said to have attributed genius about 10 percent to inspiration and 90 percent to perspiration. In other words, he appeared to believe that there is a strong positive relationship between degree of success and the amount of effort expended to achieve it. I strongly believe this also based on my own achievements and failures and those of my students. It can be both empowering and motivating for students to realize that they can significantly increase their likelihood of achieving desired goals by increasing the amount of effort that they expend to achieve them. Such a goal could be to learn the concepts and/or skills that are dealt with in a course well enough to earn a relatively high final grade in the course.

Make Students Feel That It's Safe for Them to Risk Both Answering Questions Incorrectly and Challenging Your Points of View in Class

One of my primary goals as a teacher is to enhance my students' motivation to acquire and evaluate information on their own—that is, to "turn them on" to self-learning. Consequently, I encourage them to risk in ways that are likely to facilitate their learning how to learn. One way that I do this is to encourage them to risk being wrong by volunteering to answer questions I ask in class of which they aren't 100 percent certain of the correct answer. I positively reinforce them for trying if they're wrong as long as their answer is a reasonable one based on the information they currently possess. I also encourage them to challenge my points of view if they believe they're either wrong or aren't the only possible viable ones. And if they convince me that a point of view I have is wrong or somewhat biased, I acknowledge it and use my willingness to change it as an opportunity to reinforce (in their minds) the proposition that all points of view (facts, answers) are to be regarded as tentative and subject to change whenever new information becomes available.

Increase Expectancy for Success by Increasing Experience with Success

People tend to expect events to replicate themselves. Consequently, experiencing success in learning is likely to result in an expectation of further success in learning. It's crucial, therefore, that when a student performs poorly on an examination or project you encourage him or her to attribute it to a lack of effort rather than a lack of ability (assuming, of course, that the reason for the student performing poorly isn't because he or she lacks the ability to perform well).

HOW MUCH IS IT POSSIBLE TO ENHANCE A STUDENT'S MOTIVATION TO LEARN?

Unfortunately, you won't be able to significantly enhance the motivation of all your students to learn regardless of how hard you try. And your ability to enhance the motivation of individual students will vary considerably. It's crucial that you accept your having these limitations because if you don't, you're going to find it difficult to maintain enthusiasm for teaching.

7

Making Subject Matter Seem Clear

How material is presented to students influences the amount of it they're likely to learn for at least two reasons. First, students can't learn material well unless it's presented in ways that are meaningful and clear to them. A number of factors that can affect clarity of presentation are dealt with in this chapter and some strategies for both coping with and utilizing them to enhance it are described.

A second reason why the manner in which material is presented influences the amount of it that students are likely to learn is that some students believe they can't understand material well unless it is presented to them (i.e., organized) in a particular way. Having such a certainty can discourage them from investing adequately to learn, thereby yielding a self-fulfilling prophecy. Some factors that can affect a student's confidence in his or her ability to understand course material are dealt with in this chapter and some strategies for enhancing it are described.

One reality that all instructors must face is that students differ with regard to their learning ability, learning style, and experience and these can profoundly affect their ability to understand concepts. Consequently, a "one size fits all" approach to explaining concepts is unlikely to be adequate if you really want all of your students to understand them to the extent they're capable of doing so. There are suggestions in the next section for coping with individual differences in learning ability, learning style, and experience.

COPING WITH INDIVIDUAL DIFFERENCES IN LEARNING ABILITY, LEARNING STYLE, AND EXPERIENCE

Students obviously differ in their ability to learn. Because of this, you may have to expend considerably more effort to make a concept clear to some students than to others. Many beginning instructors (as well as some experienced ones) periodically maintain eye contact with one or more of their brighter students while lecturing and when they seem to understand a concept, go on to the next one. Their doing so can have at least two undesirable consequences. First, it can result in some of their students not learning very much. And second, it can result in their receiving relatively low teaching ratings. Even their brightest students may give them low ratings because even though they're able to learn from them, they recognize that they're teaching poorly.

While all students who aren't visually or hearing impaired rely on both hearing and vision to some degree to learn from lectures, the extent to which they rely on each and the manner in which they do so can vary considerably. Some students can usually understand concepts well merely by hearing them explained. Others to understand concepts well also need to see them in printed form—for example, on overhead transparencies and/ or in handouts. Consequently, by summarizing the information needed to understand the concepts about which you're lecturing on overhead transparencies and/or in handouts, you'll probably be meeting the learning needs of more of your students.

Students also differ with regard to the extent to which they need to have the instructor organize material for them before they can learn it. Their need to have the instructor organize material is inversely related to their own ability to do so. That is, the better able they are to recognize how new material relates to what they already know, the less need they have for the instructor to help them do so. Unfortunately, some (perhaps most) students don't retain material well enough after being examined on it to develop an adequate internal structure for organizing new material completely on their own. Consequently, if you want the concepts you're presenting to be understood by as many of your students as possible, you'd be wise to present them in a highly organized way. Furthermore, if you want to maximize your teaching ratings you'd be wise to do so because there is an item on most course rating forms that pertains to how well material was organized.

Students also differ with regard to their previous experience. One variable that's likely to be relevant here is their age. I have, for example, found it to be particularly challenging in graduate classes in which I have both young adult and middle-aged students to come up with examples that are meaningful to both generations. The best way that I've found to cope with this situation is to tell students at the beginning of a course why I'll be using multiple examples and use them.

Another way that students differ with regard to experience is the amount of knowledge they already have about the concepts dealt with in a course. Some may have had courses that dealt with them or even practical experience using them. These students may seem impatient if you spend considerable time in class going over material they already know. On the hand, if some of your other students haven't been exposed previously to the subject and you aren't requiring them to have had such exposure, you're likely to anger them if you assume they have it or can compensate for their "deficiency" on their own. At least a few will probably complain about you to your chairperson or dean and/or give you relatively low teaching ratings.

FACTORS THAT CAN AFFECT CLARITY OF PRESENTATION

There are a number of factors that can affect clarity of presentation. Some are dealt with in this section. The order in which they are discussed isn't intended to indicate the amount that they're likely to do so.

Instructor's Depth of Understanding of the Material

You're unlikely to be able to explain a concept clearly if you don't really understand it. Most of my failures in making concepts clear to students resulted from my understanding of them being little more than veneer thin. While I usually use relatively simple, concrete language containing little professional jargon to explain concepts that I understand well, I tend to explain those I don't really understand well with relatively complex language that contains many highly abstract words and a great deal of professional jargon. When I do this, at least some of my students feel that their lack of understanding is their fault. I, of course, know that it's really mine, and I usually feel badly about being unable to facilitate their developing a deeper understanding of the concept.

You're likely to find it worthwhile to invest in developing a deep understanding of the concepts you attempt to teach for at least two reasons. First, it makes teaching more enjoyable. Few instructors can derive any pleasure from a classroom of students who aren't understanding what they're trying to teach. And second, it can increase your options for research and publication. The better you understand a concept (or a related set of concepts), the more likely you are to both become aware of and be able to exploit research, extramural funding, and/or publication opportunities pertaining to it.

Instructor's Use of Language

If your students don't know the meaning of some of the words you're using to explain a concept, they probably won't fully understand the concept. Consequently, if your goal is to maximize your students' understanding of what you're trying to teach rather than to impress them with the size of your vocabulary, you'd be wise to avoid using words they're unlikely to understand (particularly if you don't define them) unless you're using the words to "label" concepts you're trying to teach or to show the relationship between those concepts and others.

Instructor's Rapport with Students

The better the rapport an instructor has with his or her students, the more likely they are to expect to understand difficult concepts. When students trust an instructor to not ask them to understand concepts they're incapable of understanding, they're likely to try harder to understand them. Consequently, for teacher-student communication to be successful, you need both a teacher who is capable of explaining concepts clearly and a student who pays attention to and expects to be able to understand what the teacher is teaching.

Instructor's Use of Reinforcement and Learning Theory

Students are likely to have to struggle to understand difficult concepts well. The appropriate application of response-contingent positive reinforcement and other aspects of learning theory can increase the likelihood that they will continue to struggle long enough to do so.

Organization of Material Presented

The better organized the material that you present to students, the more likely they are to understand it. Acceptance of this relationship appears to be close to universal, judging by the fact that there is a query regarding degree of organization on almost all teaching rating forms.

Meaningfulness of Examples to Students

Examples must be meaningful to students if they are to be effective for clarifying concepts. One factor that affects their meaningfulness to students is when they were born. Examples pertaining to World War II, for example, probably were more meaningful to undergraduates 40+ years ago (when I was one) than to undergraduates now. I've taught several courses for more than 25 years and during this period I've changed several times the examples I use, in order to keep them meaningful to the generation of students I'm currently teaching.

Another factor that affects the meaningfulness of examples to students is their life experience. It can be quite challenging to find examples that are likely to be meaningful to almost all of the students in a class because of being about experiences they've had.

Degree to Which the Presentation Is Passive

Students are likely to have a more superficial understanding of concepts about which the instructor just lectures than those with which he or she also gives them the opportunity "to play." Playing with a concept can involve such activities as discussing it, answering questions about it, and/ or describing how it relates (or may relate) to other concepts. The appropriate role for an instructor while his or her students are playing with a concept in one of these ways is to give them both feedback and encouragement to keep struggling with the concept until they understand it at the depth they need to do so.

Media Employed

Some concepts can be explained more clearly by using audio- and/or video media to augment verbal descriptions of them, such as photographs, drawings, audiotapes, CD-ROM audio disks, videotapes, multimedia CD-ROM computer disks, and/or the Internet. The use of such media also helps students to understand concepts because it tends to hold their attention better than lecturing. One reason why it holds their attention is that they expect to be able to learn from such media—including television, audiotapes, videotapes, CD-ROM disks, the Internet (particularly the World Wide Web), and video games—because much of their previous learning has been from them.

FACTORS THAT CAN INFLUENCE STUDENTS' CONFIDENCE IN THEIR ABILITY TO UNDERSTAND MATERIAL

Some of the factors mentioned in the previous section that affect clarity of presentation can also affect students' confidence in their ability to understand material. Furthermore, there's "baggage" that students can bring with them to the classroom that can diminish their ability to understand it. We will focus here on the contents of such baggage.

According to the general semanticists (see Johnson, 1946), people tend to expect events to replicate themselves. Consequently, if some of your students weren't successful in the past when they tried to understand concepts of a particular type, they're likely to doubt their ability to understand others of that type. Many students in the social and behavioral sciences, for example, doubt their ability to understand mathematical concepts because of difficulty they had in the past understanding them and, as a consequence, they don't do as well as they're capable of doing in required statistics and research design courses. That is, because they anticipate being unable to understand statistical concepts, they invest little in trying to understand them and, therefore, fail to do so. Their anticipation of failing causes them to fail—that is, it yields a self-fulfilling prophecy.

The certainties in the baggage students bring with them to the classroom that interfere with their understanding material may be based more on a lack of experience than on experiencing failure. Students may believe that they're incapable of understanding certain concepts or doing certain tasks because they never really tried to understand or do them. Many people, for example, believe that they're incapable of understanding how an automobile engine functions even though they never really tried to do so. And many students are certain that they lack the ability to do publishable research even though they never had an opportunity to try.

Since certainties like those mentioned here can interfere with learning, it's important that they be identified and, if possible, challenged. Doing so in many cases will not require a referral to a therapist. You are probably capable of helping at least some of your students deal with them. There are suggestions for doing so elsewhere in this chapter. Incidentally, challenging your students in this way is likely to substantially increase the respect they have for you as a teacher and, consequently, they will probably rate your teaching more highly than they would have otherwise.

STRATEGIES FOR ENHANCING CLARITY OF PRESENTATION

A number of factors that can adversely affect clarity of presentation are considered elsewhere in this chapter. Some strategies for coping with them are suggested here. These, of course, aren't the only ones through which it's possible to enhance clarity of presentation.

Develop as Deep an Understanding of a Concept as You Can Before You Attempt to Teach It

This is more likely to be relevant for courses you're required to teach that aren't in your specialty than for those that are in it. It's particularly likely to be relevant for introductory courses that cover an entire field (e.g., introduction to psychology courses). There are bound to be at least a few concepts in such a course of which your understanding is only veneer thin. Many academics, including myself, dislike investing precious time and energy in developing a greater understanding of such concepts because doing so seems unlikely to advance our functioning as scholars and/or practitioners. However, the discomfort I experience while viewing a classroom of students looking confused and angry because I didn't understand a concept well enough to either explain it to them clearly or really answer their questions about it usually is sufficient to motivate me to try to understand the concept more deeply. Incidentally, it rarely takes me as long to do so as I thought it would. And while the investment is unlikely to enhance my functioning as a scholar, it does enhance my self-image as a teacher and, perhaps more importantly, it tends to enhance my teaching ratings.

Unless Your Goal Is to Teach Terminology, Avoid Using Words with Which Some of Your Students Are Unlikely to Be Familiar

Most of us in academia are at least a little motivated to be regarded by our students as brilliant. One way that we may, consciously or unconsciously, attempt to enhance our image of being so is to exhibit a very large vocabulary. That is, rather than explaining concepts using relatively common words that all of our students will understand, we may do so using a number of less common ones that at least a few of our students are unlikely to understand. We can, of course, attribute their lack of understanding to a deficiency in them rather than in our teaching. And we may be right. However, the reality is that our students' vocabulary is what it is. And while we certainly should do everything that we can to encourage them to expand it, if we really want them to learn maximally from us, we'll have to explain concepts to them in language that they're able to understand. Furthermore, if we want them to give us decent teaching ratings, we'll have to do the same thing.

Relate to Your Students as a Person Rather than as an Information-Providing Entity

Students are more highly motivated to please instructors whom they regard as persons than those they regard as entities. And the more highly motivated they are to please an instructor, the harder they're likely to struggle to understand the concepts that he or she tries to teach them.

Some of the ways that you may be able to get students to view you as a person rather than an entity include the following:

- Show them that you have a good sense of humor.
- Evince interest in them as people (e.g., learn their names and wish them a nice vacation at the end of the last class before a vacation begins).
- Talk *to* them rather than *at* them by doing such things as maintaining eye contact with them while lecturing.

- Encourage them to ask questions and to disagree with your points of view.
- Encourage them to visit you during your office hours if there are ways you can be helpful to them.
- Indicate to them that all of the "facts" you present are tentative and subject to change whenever new relevant information becomes available.
- Occasionally tell them about a "dumb thing" you've done (one, of course, that's unlikely to cause them to question your competence).

These are merely suggestions. All of them may not be compatible with your personality. There are, undoubtedly, other things you can do that will accomplish the same end.

Use Response-Contingent Positive Reinforcement to Encourage Students to Persist in Their Struggle to Understand Difficult Concepts Well

An adage in which there is a great deal of truth is that nothing succeeds like success nor fails like failure. By providing the type of positive reinforcement that causes students to believe they're making progress toward gaining a deeper understanding of a concept, you'll increase the likelihood that they'll continue in their quest to develop a deeper understanding of it. There is, incidentally, a huge literature dealing with the impact of response-contingent positive reinforcement on learning.

Define Terminology Extensionally Whenever Possible

You define a term extensionally by presenting (pointing to) the unit of experience to which it refers rather than using words to describe or explain it. Defining an object by presenting it to students is more likely to convey a true impression of its appearance and function than is describing it with words. As the adage suggests, a picture is worth a thousand words. Likewise, causing students to experience what a term (concept) refers to is more likely to convey a real understanding of its meaning than is describing it. For example, I require my students (who are majoring in speech-language pathology) to simulate a speech disorder outside of class in at least three situations so that they can learn firsthand how people react to persons who have such a disorder.

Organize the Material You're Using to Explain a Concept in a Way That's Likely to Make It Relatively Easy for Students to Understand

One approach I've found useful for organizing material to explain a concept is based on a scheme I learned while an undergraduate at Emerson

College that was referred to as the Evolution of Expression. According to this scheme, teaching students to understand a concept (or to perfect a skill) is a four-stage process in which the depth of understanding (or refinement of the skill) at Stage Four is considerably greater than that at Stage One. The four stages are:

- Stage One: The whole
- Stage Two: The parts
- Stage Three: The parts in relation to the whole
- Stage Four: The parts in relation to each other

You begin by defining the concept (with words and/or extensionally) in a way that's likely to provide students with an overview or intuitive understanding of both the territory (i.e., unit of experience) for which it serves as a map and how it relates to other concepts in the field. You then define the entities that form the territory (with words and/or extensionally), describe their relationship to the territory as a whole, and, finally, describe the manner in which they affect (i.e., interact with) each other.

To illustrate this process, suppose that the concept you're teaching is the function of the brain. You'd begin with an overview of what the brain does and how it interacts with other structures in the body. You would then describe the function of each of its components (e.g., the cerebrum and cerebellum). Next, you would indicate how each component contributes to the functioning of the brain as a whole. And finally, you would indicate how the individual components of the brain interact with each other.

Use Examples That Are Likely to Be Meaningful to Your Students

If you're at the beginning of your teaching career, you're less likely to have difficulty coming up with examples that are meaningful to your students than you are if you're, like me, near the end of it. The reason is that you're closer in age to your students, and consequently, your life experience is more similar to theirs than is mine. People who were regarded as superstars by my generation, for example, aren't regarded so by theirs. In fact, at least some of the current crop of students wouldn't even recognize their names. Consequently, examples based on them would be meaningless now to many students. The same would be true for at least some of the events that were very meaningful to persons of my generation, including the Depression and World War II. You should, therefore, plan to change your examples from time to time as the distance between your generation and that of your students increases.

Provide Opportunities for Students to "Play" with the Concepts You're Trying to Help Them Understand

Giving students opportunities to play with or apply a concept is likely to make it clearer to them than just listening to you lecture about it. Several activities that can enable them to do so are the following:

- Asking and answering questions about the concept.
- Attempting to explain the concept or teach it to someone.
- Attempting to apply the concept to situations or scenarios that weren't discussed in class.
- Attempting to assess the concept's validity and/or that of criticisms of it.

These, of course, are not the only such activities.

Use Media Other than Lecturing by You to Explain a Concept When Doing So Is Likely to Help Students Understand It

Such media could include photographs, drawings, films, videotapes, audiotapes, CD-ROM disks, and computer-based tutorials and multimedia presentations. They could also include readings (in books and/or journals) and guest speakers (particularly ones who are more knowledgeable than you about the subject).

Tell Them What You're Going to Tell Them, Tell Them, and Tell Them What You Told Them

The proper use of this formula increases the likelihood that a concept will be understood because students will be exposed at least three times to the essential information needed to understand it.

STRATEGIES OF INCREASING STUDENTS' CONFIDENCE IN THEIR ABILITY TO UNDERSTAND A CONCEPT

One of my professors (the late Wendell Johnson of the University of Iowa) once commented to me and several of his other graduate assistants that a characteristic of a great teacher is that he or she gets students to understand and/or perform at levels at which they didn't believe previously they were capable of understanding or performing. This comment influenced profoundly how I tried to be helpful to students throughout my teaching career.

One block to learning a student can have is a *certainty* that he or she lacks the ability to understand a concept. I describe here an approach (strategy) for coping with such a block. For further information about the rationale for the approach and ways to implement it, see Johnson (1946).

Increase Students' Awareness of the Source(s) from Which Their Lack of Confidence in Their Ability to Understand the Concept Arises

The reason of their lack of confidence is most likely to be one or more previous attempts to understand this or a similar concept (or concepts) that they don't regard as having been successful. They may either have been unsuccessful in understanding the concept(s) or they may not have been as successful as they expected to be, and because they're perfectionistic, they didn't regard the level of understanding they achieved as being successful. Regardless of which is true, their expectation of failure can keep them from really trying to understand the concept, thereby producing a self-fulfilling prophecy.

By encouraging students to answer one or more of the following questions for themselves, you may be able to help them become more aware of why they doubt their ability to understand a particular concept:

- On a scale from 1 to 10, with 1 being no confidence and 10 being high confidence, how confident are you that you're capable of learning this concept?
- If your rating was lower than 10, what was the reason?
- Have you previously tried to learn this or similar concepts and were unsuccessful? If yes, how old were you and what were the circumstances?
- In what ways are you and the circumstances different now from what you and they were then?
- Could you have been unsuccessful in understanding the concept at least in part because you expected to be unsuccessful?

You could either pose these questions in class or during office hours to individual students who would be likely to benefit from this kind of soul-searching because of having such a certainty.

Challenge Students to Test Their Certainty That They're Incapable of Understanding the Concept

A student who believes that he or she lacks the ability *now* to understand a particular concept (or class of concepts) may be wrong. There's only one way for him or her to find out—that is, to consider the certainty to be a hypothesis and test it according to the rules of the scientific method. Such a test, if it is to yield an outcome that is free of bias, must be one in which the student assumes neither success nor failure before doing it, "at a gut level." Assuming failure, of course, could result in a self-fulfilling prophecy, thereby biasing the results of the test. The potential benefits that a student could derive from doing such a test are likely to far outweigh any negative consequences to him or her. The worst case scenario would be that the student confirms his or her belief in being unable to understand the concept. While this outcome could cause the student to be depressed for a few days, it would be highly unlikely to injure him or her long term.

The likelihood that such a test will yield a positive outcome is inversely related to the degree to which the student is perfectionistic. While a student who isn't perfectionistic is likely to interpret even a relatively small increase in his or her ability to understand a concept as success, a student who is highly perfectionistic is unlikely to interpret anything but a relatively large one in this way. And, of course, relatively small increases in understanding tend to occur more often than relatively large ones.

Present the Concept to Students in Ways That Maximize Their Likelihood of Understanding It When They Test Their Certainty That They're Incapable of Doing So

The clearer a concept is presented, the greater the likelihood that it will be understood. There are a number of suggestions for maximizing clarity of presentation elsewhere in this chapter. Also, the more willing students are to regard relatively small increases in their ability to understand a concept as being successful, the more likely they are to conclude that they do have the ability to understand it.

Challenge Students to Identify and Test Other Certainties That Are Detrimental to Them

Almost everyone has certainties that are handicapping. That is, they have certainties that keep them from trying and/or being successful doing things they'd like to do. When your students' attempts to test this certainty result in it being rejected, you may want to motivate them to identify and test other certainties that limit their potential to contribute to society, enjoy life, or both.

8

Demonstrating Concern and Respect for Students

Do unto others as you would have them do unto you.
—The Golden Rule

There are many things teachers do in and out of the classroom that can affect students' perceptions of the concern and respect they have for them. Some of the issues that were dealt with in both previous chapters and will be dealt with in subsequent ones can affect their perceptions of both, at least indirectly. We will focus in this chapter on some of the possible impacts that demonstrating concern and respect for students can have on both students and teachers and on some do's, don'ts, and maybes for doing so. Almost all of the do's, don'ts, and maybes, incidentally, were abstracted from interviews with students.

HOW DEMONSTRATING CONCERN AND RESPECT FOR STUDENTS CAN IMPACT ON BOTH YOU AND THEM

Your ability to be helpful to students will be affected by the amount of concern and respect that they believe you have for them as learners and as people. Students are more likely to both pay attention to and attempt to please teachers whom they believe really care about and respect them than they are those whom they believe have little or no real interest to them. They're also more likely to use teachers as role models whom they believe really care about and respect them.

Demonstrating concern and respect for students can also benefit you in several ways. First, and perhaps most important, it will probably increase your student teaching rating for this item. And the increase may not be limited to just this item. When students believe that an instructor really cares about them as people, they tend to rate all aspects of his or her teaching at least a little higher than they would otherwise. Conversely, when students believe that an instructor cares little about them as people, they're likely to rate almost all aspects of his or her teaching at least a little lower than otherwise. Consequently, not demonstrating adequate concern and respect for students could considerably lower your overall teaching ratings, thereby keeping you, at the very least, from being awarded promotion and tenure early (i.e., before the end of your probationary period). As I've indicated previously, college promotion and tenure committees hesitate to tenure persons early whose teaching appears to be in considerable need of improvement because they believe that their refusal to do so provides an incentive for them to improve their teaching.

Another way that you can benefit by demonstrating concern and respect for students is by your teaching and other interactions with them being more pleasant than they would tend to be otherwise. There are several ways this could happen. First, they could be pleasant to you more often, both inside and outside of the classroom. Second, they could reveal themselves to you as people more frequently and if you're a "people person," you'd probably find their doing so enjoyable. Third, they'd complain about you and your teaching less to other faculty, students, your chairperson, and/or your dean. And fourth, they'd be more likely to strongly support your receiving teaching awards and tenure.

DO'S

These suggestions were abstracted from interviews with approximately 40 undergraduate and graduate students. The students were asked to indicate ways professors have treated them that caused them to believe that they really cared about and respected them. The order in which the suggestions are listed isn't intended to indicate the amount they're likely to impact on students' perceptions of concern and respect.

Communicate Looking Forward to Having the Opportunity to Teach Them

You should communicate this message, both verbally and non-verbally, whenever you begin a course. To do it verbally, you would say it in a way that, with your personality, would seem sincere. And to do it non-verbally, you could evince enthusiasm for the course.

Treat Students as People, Not Just as Course Enrollees

It's easy to view students, particularly ones in large lecture courses, as items on an enrollment sheet rather than as persons. By doing so, you're likely to dehumanize your treatment of them, at least a little. While it's admittedly difficult to treat students in large lecture courses as persons rather than items, it can be done. There are at least a few instructors at every college who are able to do this. They are ones who almost always have large enrollments in the electives they teach for nonmajors.

Let Students Be Themselves and Respect Them as Such

The more similar your students' learning style and motivation are to yours, the easier it will be for you to accept and respect them. Some of your students will probably differ considerably from you with regard to one or both of them. You are likely to have a tendency, which may be either conscious or unconscious, to expect students to conform to what you perceive as being an appropriate learning style and level of motivation and only show respect for them if they do so. Your pressuring them to conform in these ways is not only likely to reduce your teaching ratings but also, and perhaps more importantly, reduce the likelihood that you'll contribute significantly to your students becoming all that they can be.

One of the main differences between an adequate teacher and a great teacher is that the latter allows students to be themselves and respects and encourages them to be so. Who are the teachers who impacted on you the most? Did they do so, at least in part, because they accepted and respected you as you were?

Expect the Best, but Don't Expect the Impossible

What would constitute expecting improvement for one student would constitute expecting the impossible for another. Students differ in their ability to learn to do tasks and understand concepts. What would be a relatively high level of performing or understanding for one student may be a relatively low one for another. We should show students respect who perform up to their potential, regardless of what it is. And we should encourage students to perform better if they have the ability to do so, regardless of how well they perform.

Help Students Learn How to Teach Themselves

Learning is a life-long process. Once students graduate, they'll have the primary responsibility for teaching themselves. One way to show respect for students is to provide opportunities and support for them to experience success in doing so.

If You're Teaching a Course in Which There Are Both Majors and Non-Majors, Treat the Non-Majors with the Same Respect That You Treat the Majors

Your failing to do this can reduce your teaching ratings. It can also reduce the motivation of at least a few of the students who aren't majors to do well in the course. Furthermore, particularly if this is an introductory lower division undergraduate course, it can reduce the likelihood that some of those who aren't majors will be turned on sufficiently to your field to be motivated to major in it. For the past 25 years, at least a third of our undergraduate students have declared our department as their major after taking our introductory course.

Recognize and React Appropriately to Differences in Students' Needs for Help and Reinforcement

Students differ in what they need from us to learn to the maximum extent to which they're capable. Some will need practically no assistance or encouragement (reinforcement) from us to learn to do a particular task or understand a particular concept and others a great deal. If we really respect and want to be helpful to all of our students, therefore, we'll recognize and react appropriately to differences in their needs for help and reinforcement.

Communicate with Language That All of Your Students Can Understand

Presentations to peers are a more appropriate venue for exhibiting the size of your vocabulary than are lectures to students. For students to learn from you, they must be able to understand what you say to them. Consequently, unless you're teaching terminology, you should try to avoid using words with which at least some of them are unlikely to be familiar.

Begin and End Classes on Time

Students tend to question the concern and respect that instructors have for them if they're frequently late to class and/or fail to end classes on time. They assume that if they can get to class on time, the instructor should be able to also. They're particularly likely to question an instructor's concern and respect for them if he or she doesn't end classes on time. They may have a class the next hour in a different building and not ending a class on time can cause them to be late. Even a single such experience could cause a student to lower the teaching ratings that he or she gives an instructor considerably.

Recognize Individual Differences in the Amount of Time It Takes Students to Complete Examinations and Make Certain That There's Adequate Time for the Slower Students to Complete Them

A student can do poorly on an exam because he or she lacks information, or because he or she works relatively slowly and doesn't have time to finish, or both. Since the purpose of an examination is usually to find how much a student knows rather than how quickly he or she can answer questions, it's important that examinations be short enough to allow students who work a little more slowly than others to complete them. Failing to do so is failing to accept the fact that degree of understanding and speed of responding are not necessarily highly correlated.

If Students Ask Questions During a Lecture, Answer Them if You Can When They Are Asked Rather than Putting Off Doing So Until Some Future Time

It's tempting to put off answering questions while you're lecturing because stopping to do so can break your train of thought. While this is true, the consequences of not doing so can be worse. It can result in at least one student not really understanding what you're trying to communicate.

Another problem with delaying answering questions until the end is that you may not have time to answer them or forget to answer them. Not doing so could impede learning and be interpreted as being indicative of a lack of concern for students.

Give Students Plenty of Advanced Notice if Examination Dates or Project Due Dates Are Not Those Indicated in the Syllabus

Perhaps nothing infuriates students more than an instructor changing examination or project due dates in the syllabus without giving them plenty of advanced notice. And even if you give it to them, you're going to have to be flexible in dealing with the problems the change causes if you want them to continue to believe that you're concerned about their welfare.

Grade Examinations and Projects Quickly and Let Students Know Their Grades

For students to do well on the examinations and projects in a course, they must be knowledgeable about what the professor expects. To determine whether their assumptions about this are "on target," they need feed-back. The quicker they get it, the more time they have to adjust if they aren't "on target."

Have a Review Session Before Examinations

Some students tend to assume that instructors who have review sessions before examinations really care about them. Scheduling such sessions is also desirable for another reason. It can facilitate learning. That is, attending a review session can give a student who didn't understand a concept well when it was presented another opportunity to grasp it.

While Lecturing, Stop Periodically and Ask if There Are Any Questions

This is another way by which you can communicate to students that you really care about them. Your doing so can also cause them to pay more attention in class than they would otherwise, thereby enhancing learning.

Learn Students' Names

Almost all students base some of their judgments of how much instructors are concerned about and respect them on whether they learn their names. Not learning them is almost certain to reduce your teaching ratings, except possibly in huge lecture courses.

Really Listen to Students and Be Respectful of Their Opinions if They Differ from Yours

We all like it when others share our opinions, and when they don't, our natural tendency is to be defensive. If you want students to believe that you're respectful of them and their opinions, you'll have to counter this tendency and listen carefully to why their opinions differ from yours. You can then debate with them the virtues of both. The result could be their changing their opinion to yours, your changing your opinion to theirs, or you both respectfully agreeing to disagree.

Some instructors, incidentally, hesitate admitting being wrong to students because they assume that their doing so will cause students to respect them less. Actually, the opposite is more likely. Students tend to respect instruc-tors who are willing to admit being wrong, particularly if they do so as a result of input from students.

Encourage Students to Make Appointments to See You During Your Office Hours if They're Having any Course-Related Problems

Making yourself available to students is almost always interpreted by them as evidence of concern and respect. Of course, how you treat them when they come to see you will also influence their judgment about these.

When You List Your Office Hours, Indicate That You're Also Available "by Appointment"

One of the surprises from my interviewing students was the strong feelings many expressed about being able to meet with an instructor at times other than those indicated for office hours. Their class or work schedule may preclude their meeting with him or her at any of the times listed. Even if they never have to meet with an instructor outside of class, the fact that the instructor is sufficiently flexible to enable them to do so communicates that he or she really cares about them.

Encourage Students to Communicate with You by E-Mail About any Course-Related Problems

Doing so is likely to communicate concern and respect for them, provided that you also give them the option of seeing you at your office.

Be Flexible When Scheduling Examinations

Flexibility is likely to be viewed by students as evidence of concern and respect. The need for flexibility when scheduling exams applies to both entire classes and individuals. You may not, for example, want to schedule an exam the same day that another instructor in your department who has many of the same students has already done so. And you may want to allow students who have valid reasons for doing so to take examinations at times other than those at which they're scheduled.

Be Flexible with Students Who Miss Class Occasionally Because of Participation in Sports or Other Extracurricular Activities

Students who have to miss class occasionally because of participation in team sports and other official extracurricular activities (e.g., band) are almost certain to hate you if you don't give them the opportunity to make up the work they've missed. If your course is such that work from missing classes cannot be made up, you should announce this *the first day of class* so that students who know they'll be missing classes will still be able to drop your course and take another.

Attempt to Be Helpful to Students Whose Learning Styles Differ from Yours

Your expressing a willingness to do this and doing it is highly likely to be interpreted by students, even ones whose learning style is similar to yours, as demonstrating concern and respect for them.

Make Students Believe That You Really Want Them to Understand What You're Attempting to Teach

You can communicate to students that you really want them to understand a concept by using language to explain it they're able to understand and examples that are likely to be meaningful to them because they're based on things they've experienced. You can also communicate this to students by giving them opportunities *before* testing them on a concept to explain it to you and/or apply it.

Make Students Feel Comfortable Admitting That They Don't Understand a Concept and Asking for Further Explanation

One way to make students feel comfortable admitting that they don't really understand a concept (particularly if it is a relatively abstract one) is by telling them that the concept is difficult to understand and indicating that you had to struggle to understand it.

DON'TS

These suggestions were also abstracted from interviews with approximately 40 undergraduate and graduate students. The students were asked to indicate ways professors have treated them that caused them to believe they didn't really care about or respect them. The order in which the suggestions are listed isn't intended to indicate the amount they're likely to impact on students' perceptions of lack of concern and/or respect.

Don't Talk Down to Students or Be Rude to Them

College students are unlikely to believe that an instructor respects them if he or she talks to or otherwise treats them like young children or persons who are borderline mentally retarded. Nor are they likely to regard an instructor who is rude to them as someone who really cares about or respects them.

Don't Lecture at Students

The goal of lecturing should not be self-stimulation but sharing knowledge. It's difficult to communicate to students if you don't, for example, maintain eye contact with them. We've all attended sessions at professional meetings at which we felt we were being lectured at rather than to. We are particularly likely to feel this way if a speaker reads his or her remarks and, consequently, maintains poor eye contact with us.

Don't Overly Focus Your Teaching on Your Research

Students are likely to assume that their instructors care more about their research than they do about them. This isn't particularly surprising considering the weight most institutions give to excellence in research as compared to what they give to excellence in teaching for promotion and tenure decisions. Focusing on your research, when the relevance of doing so isn't obvious, can have a detrimental impact on your teaching ratings by reinforcing this belief.

Students may also interpret your overly focusing on your research as "patting yourself on the back" (i.e., a lack of humility) or being unwilling to spend time preparing for class. Either of these interpretations could cause them to give you lower teaching ratings than they would otherwise.

Don't Go to Class Unprepared

One of the best ways to communicate to students that you care little about them and don't really respect them is to frequently go to class unprepared.

Don't Always Conduct Classes Exactly the Same Way

Students are likely to assume that if you always conduct classes exactly the same way and it isn't because of the nature of the course, the reason is you don't want to spend any more time preparing than absolutely necessary. While varying how you do so will require at least a small investment of time and energy, the payoff can be substantial both for your teaching ratings and students' learning.

Don't Base Course Grades, if Possible, on Only One or Two Tests and/or Projects

Students may assume if you base their final grade in a course on only one or two test/project grades that it's because you don't want to spend time grading more of them. Their making such an assumption could obviously cause them to lower the ratings they give your teaching, particularly if they believe (rightly or wrongly) that their final grade would be higher if it were based on more test/project grades. Issues concerning grading are dealt with further in Chapter 12.

Don't Schedule Examinations at the End of a Class During Which You'll Be Lecturing

Comments from several students suggested that they don't regard an instructor as being sensitive to their feelings if he or she schedules an examination at the end of a class. Because they are experiencing anxiety about the examination, they tend to retain little of what precedes it. They're particularly likely to question an instructor's concern for them if some of the material on which they're being tested is presented at the same session as the examination. Examination administration issues are dealt with further in Chapter 12.

Don't Schedule an Examination a Day or Two After Students Return from Vacation

This was mentioned by a number of students. They indicated that having to spend a lot of time studying during a vacation because an examination was scheduled for a day or two after it resulted in the vacation ceasing to be one. Their resentment about this could cause them to question your caring about them and, consequently, adversely affect the teaching ratings they give you. It would be particularly likely to do so if it was a vacation that occurred shortly before the rating task was administered (e.g., the Thanksgiving vacation for colleges on the semester system).

Don't Speak So Fast While Lecturing That Some of Your Students Won't Be Able to Take Adequate Notes

A common complaint of students about instructors is that they speak too rapidly for them to take adequate notes. I experienced this frustration frequently while I was a student. If only a few of the students in a class appear to be having difficulty taking notes for this reason, you may want to suggest to them that they tape-record your lectures.

Don't Accelerate the Rate at Which You Present Material at the End of a Course

It's important to pace yourself so that you present approximately the same amount of material during each session of a course. If your pace is too slow for the first two-thirds or so of a course, you're likely to feel compelled to accelerate it to be able to cover all the material that you want and/or need to cover. A number of students whom we interviewed felt that it was unfair for an instructor to expect them to learn huge amounts of material near the end of a course for this reason. If many of the students in a course felt this way, the result could be your receiving lower teaching ratings for it than otherwise.

Don't Cut Fruitful Discussions Short Because Allowing Them to Continue Interferes with Your Covering All of the Material You Wanted to Cover

During my more than 30 years of college teaching, the classes from which both me and my students probably learned the most were ones during which at least a few students were sufficiently aroused (provoked) by something I said to want to discuss it. While a point can be reached in any discussion when it makes sense to terminate it because participants are saying the same things over and over again, it can take a while to get to this point. I'd rather present a little less material in a course and have a little more of what I do present really impact on students' attitudes and understanding of concepts. Furthermore, by encouraging class discussions, I'm communicating to my students that I really respect their opinions, thereby possibly enhancing the teaching ratings they give me.

When Students Come to Your Office During Your Office Hours, Try Not to Communicate (Verbally or Nonverbally) That You're Too Busy to Talk to Them

One way that we communicate this to students nonverbally is by not giving them our full attention. Students could, of course, interpret our not doing so as not respecting them. I've found it best when I can't give a student my full attention to be honest about it and arrange another time to meet with him or her.

Don't Pass Back Examinations in Class in Grade Order

It never would have occurred to me to include this if I hadn't interviewed students about what instructors do that demonstrate a lack of concern and respect for them. Apparently, some instructors who pass back examinations in class, order them by grade before doing so. While this practice may be highly reinforcing to those who receive relatively high grades, it can be humiliating to those who don't. Both the students who feel humiliated and some of their friends are likely to interpret your passing back examinations this way as demonstrating a lack of concern and respect for students and rate your teaching accordingly.

Don't Show Favoritism

While the recipients of your favoritism are likely to rate your teaching highly, most of the others are likely to do the opposite, particularly if your show of favoritism is blatant. Furthermore, your doing so could anger your chairperson or dean sufficiently for one or both of them to not support your bid for promotion and tenure. Such a scenario would be particularly likely if they frequently had to deal with legitimate complaints from students about your showing favoritism.

Don't Try to Trick Students on Exams—Test Them Straightforwardly on What They're Supposed to Know

A good way to anger students is to have them do poorly on an examination because of the way it was constructed. Questions may be worded, for example, in ways that would tend to make a test as much (or more) one of intelligence as of knowledge. Issues related to test construction are dealt with in Chapter 12.

Don't Read and React to Students' Answers While They Are Writing Them During Examinations

Some instructors walk around the room while monitoring an examination and read and react, verbally and/or nonverbally, to students' answers while they're writing them. Several of the students whom we interviewed mentioned that they found their doing so disturbing.

If Possible, Avoid Grading on a Bell-Shaped Curve When It Results in Students Getting Lower Grades than They Would Have Otherwise

At least a few of your students who receive a lower grade on an examination than they would have if you didn't "grade on a curve" are likely to question your concern about them. It can be argued that a grade should reflect the amount a student has learned rather than the amount that both the student and his or her classmates have learned. This issue is dealt with in Chapter 12.

MAYBES

These suggestions, like the preceding ones, were abstracted from interviews with approximately 40 undergraduate and graduate students who were asked to indicate ways professors have treated them that caused them to believe they really cared about and respected them. They're classified as maybes because they could be either do's or don'ts. The order in which they are listed isn't intended to indicate the amount they're likely to impact on students' perceptions of concern and respect.

Socialize with Students Outside of Class

While doing so can communicate your really caring about and respecting students as people, it can also lead to charges of favoritism and other undesirable consequences. It would be less risky to do with graduate students than with undergraduates and with groups of students than with individual ones.

Include Your Home Telephone Number on Your Syllabi

Students are likely to appreciate your allowing them to phone you at home, particularly if there are days you don't come to campus. However, whether it's a good idea to encourage them to do so depends, in large part, on how the persons with whom you live feel about it. If your spouse, for example, strongly objects to your counseling students or dealing with their problems while at home, it probably wouldn't be a good idea to include your home telephone number on your syllabi.

Allow Students to Argue for the Correctness of Their Answers on Essay Tests

I don't encourage students to do this unless they're almost certain I graded a question incorrectly. However, a few of the students whom we interviewed mentioned that they had had professors who encouraged them to do this and that they were appreciative of having this option. Be aware if you're going to encourage students to do this that it can be time consuming and that they're likely to become infuriated with you if you don't accept their arguments.

Give Students Alternative Ways to Earn a Course Grade

I've never done this, but several students mentioned having instructors who did and really appreciated their doing so. Whether it makes sense to give students this option would depend on the nature of the course and the number of students enrolled. If a course has a small enrollment, for example, you might offer students the option of taking an oral examination rather than a written one.

Have Extra Credit Questions on Examinations or Extra Credit Assignments

Students tend to appreciate such options. However, whether it's sensible to offer them depends on the nature and difficulty of the course. I'm most likely to offer them when they have the potential to facilitate students' understanding of what I'm trying to teach.

WHAT WOULD YOU LIKE YOUR OBITUARY TO SAY ABOUT YOU AS A TEACHER?

A motivational speaker whom I heard on television a while back suggested that people write an obituary that says what they'd like theirs to say and then do what they can to maximize the odds it will say it. With regard to your functioning as a teacher, what would you like your obituary to say? I'd like mine to say that I impacted significantly on my students' lives. Of course, you'd be highly unlikely to be able to have such an impact without showing genuine concern and respect for them.

9

Communicating Enthusiasm for a Course

For teaching, enthusiasm is everything. It's the factor that the students whom we interviewed mentioned most often as profoundly affecting their ratings of teachers. While the presence of enthusiasm doesn't necessarily cause students to consider an instructor a good teacher, the absence of enthusiasm almost always causes them to consider him or her a poor one.

You're highly unlikely to be able to communicate enthusiasm for teaching a course if you don't genuinely feel enthusiastic about teaching it. There are a number of reasons why an instructor may lack enthusiasm for teaching a particular course or for teaching in general. Some of them are considered in this chapter along with possible remedies.

FACTORS THAT CAN AFFECT ENTHUSIASM FOR TEACHING

A number of factors that can affect enthusiasm for teaching are discussed in this section. The order in which they're discussed is not intended to specify the amount that each is likely to impact on it.

Commitment to Teaching

Commitment to teaching usually translates into enthusiasm for teaching. The degree of commitment to teaching can vary from it being considered a necessary evil if you want to be a scholar to it being the primary reason for wanting to be on a college faculty. It can also vary based on the type and level of teaching. A person may have a stronger commitment to teaching clinical skills by supervising student practicum than by teaching lecture courses dealing with them. Or a person may have a stronger commitment to teaching graduate students than to teaching lower division undergraduate ones.

Enthusiasm of Your Mentors for Teaching

Persons who were physically or psychologically abused as children are more likely to abuse their own children than they would be otherwise. They're mimicking the model to which they were exposed without probably being fully conscious of doing so. Similarly, instructors whose mentors lacked enthusiasm for teaching certain kinds of courses are more likely to lack enthusiasm for teaching them than they would otherwise. They also would be mimicking the model to which they were exposed without probably being fully conscious of doing so. A different outcome would, of course, be likely if their mentors had exhibited genuine enthusiasm for teaching.

Attitudes of the Chairperson and Senior Faculty in the Department Toward Teaching

If the chairperson and/or senior faculty in a department lack genuine enthusiasm for teaching, the junior faculty are also likely to lack it for at least two reasons. First, the chairperson and/or senior faculty are likely to positively reinforce enthusiasm for other aspects of the job, such as publishing and grant getting. Second, they're likely to punish enthusiasm for good teaching, particularly if it results in significantly lower enrollments in their elective courses. Our student surveys revealed that the enthusiasm of the instructor frequently tends to be as important a consideration as content when students are selecting elective courses.

Pressure to Secure Extramural Funding and to Publish

The greater the pressure to secure extramural funding and to publish, the less time and energy a faculty member is likely to have available to invest in teaching and, consequently, the less enthusiasm he or she is likely to have for doing it. Those who aren't high energy and/or are married and have children are particularly likely to lack enthusiasm for teaching for this reason.

Previous Experiences with Teaching

If your previous experiences with teaching a particular course or group of students or with teaching in general weren't enjoyable, you're likely to be less enthusiastic about teaching than you'd be otherwise. In fact, unless you're a masochist, your tendency will be to invest as little of yourself as you can in teaching. While doing so may help to protect your ego, it's unlikely to enhance your chances for promotion and tenure.

Reactions of Previous Students

It's difficult to be enthusiastic about teaching a course if the students didn't respond positively when you taught it previously. If they did do so, however, you're likely to be enthusiastic about teaching it again.

If you feel that the students didn't responded positively when you taught a course previously, you can easily get into a "seek and ye shall find" situation when you teach it again. That is, you're likely to search for evidence that they aren't responding positively and your doing so can easily trigger a self-fulfilling prophecy.

Reactions of Current Students

My enthusiasm during any moment while teaching a class is affected profoundly by how my students are responding to what I'm saying. If they seem interested and enthusiastic, my level of enthusiasm is likely to be relatively high. On the other hand, if they appear to have little or no interest in what I'm saying, my level of enthusiasm is likely to diminish. And as mine diminishes, whatever they have usually does also.

Attitude Toward Teaching Particular Course Content

It's easier to be enthusiastic while teaching some kinds of material than it is while teaching others. I am, for example, more likely to be perceived as being highly enthusiastic when teaching material in a field that I've done research than I am when teaching material in a field that I don't now have nor have ever had a research interest.

Family and Other External Responsibilities

Your life outside of academia can profoundly affect your life within it. College faculty, like all human beings, have available only a finite amount of time and energy and the more of it that they have to invest outside of academia, the less they'll have to invest within it. And with the pressure they're likely to feel to publish and seek extramural funding, the aspect of their job responsibilities that's probably most likely to suffer is teaching. It would, of course, be difficult to be enthusiastic about teaching if you knew that you didn't have the time and/or energy to do what's necessary to do it well.

Unrealistic Expectations for Students Acknowledging and Appreciating Your Efforts to Teach Them

You can lose enthusiasm for teaching if your expectations for students acknowledging and appreciating your efforts are unrealistic. This is one of the most frequent reasons (perhaps the most frequent) for faculty losing "fire," or enthusiasm, for teaching. The stronger your expectation that students will say something or otherwise acknowledge and appreciate your efforts to teach them if they do so, the more likely you are to feel unappreciated as a teacher and, consequently, the more difficult it will be for you to continue being enthusiastic about teaching.

Fatigue and "Burnout"

It's difficult to be enthusiastic about anything when your energy level is low. A low energy level can result from fatigue, such as that symptomatic of certain physiological disorders (e.g., fibromyalgia) and psychological ones (e.g., chronic depression). It can also result from "burnout."

STRATEGIES THAT CAN INCREASE ENTHUSIASM FOR TEACHING

There are a number of things you can do that may enable you to increase your enthusiasm for teaching. Some are described in this section. The order in which they're dealt with isn't intended to indicate either their likelihood of being successful or the amount of enthusiasm they're likely to generate.

Avoid Unrealistic Expectations

Don't assume that your students' failure to thank you for your teaching efforts means that they aren't appreciated. I've been teaching for more than 30 years and am a recipient of my university's annual faculty award for teaching excellence. Yet, I can count on the fingers of both hands the number of times that a student who is a U.S. citizen has gone out of their way to thank me. My experience with my Palestinian and other foreign students, incidentally, has been quite different in this regard.

Increase Your Awareness of the Possible Rewards from Teaching Well

The stronger your belief that teaching well yields rewards that are commensurate with the investments required for doing so, the more likely you are to be enthusiastic about teaching. One way that you may be able to increase your awareness of the possible rewards from teaching well is by answering the following hypothetical questions:

- If you were to invest sufficiently in your teaching to do it well, in what specific ways would *you* be likely to benefit?
- If you were to invest sufficiently in your teaching to do it well, in what specific ways would *your students* be likely to benefit?
- If you were to invest sufficiently in your teaching to do it well, in what specific ways would *society* be likely to benefit?

It's likely to take more than a few minutes of soul searching to adequately answer these questions.

Don't Expect Situations to Replicate Themselves

Don't assume because students gave you poor teaching ratings the last time you taught a particular course that they'll do it again. The students won't be the same and you probably won't teach the course in exactly the same way. Furthermore, such an expectation can affect your teaching in ways that are likely to result in a self-fulfilling prophecy.

Find Reasons to Increase Your Commitment to Teaching

The stronger your commitment to teaching, the better you'll probably teach and, consequently, the more enthusiastic you'll probably be about teaching. The way to do this, as I've indicated previously, is to become more aware of how you, your students, and society are likely to benefit from your having such a commitment.

Get to Know Your Students as People

It is much easier to be enthusiastic while teaching *John* and *Mary* than it is while teaching *students*. The better you get to know your students as people, the more likely they are to attend and be receptive to what you teach and, consequently, the more likely you are to be enthusiastic while teaching them.

Increase Your Students' Awareness of the Relevance of the Material You're Teaching

Your students' enthusiasm for your teaching is likely to affect yours. Consequently, getting them to regard what you're teaching as relevant is likely to increase their enthusiasm for learning it, thereby increasing your enthusiasm for teaching it.

One mistake instructors frequently make is assuming that the relevance of the material they're teaching is obvious to students because it's obvious to them. However, they know what comes later that makes it relevant, but at least some of their students may not.

Become More Knowledgeable About the Subject Matter of the Courses You Teach

It's more difficult to be enthusiastic about teaching material about which your knowledge is veneer thin than it is that about which you're knowledgeable. Consequently, you may be able to increase your enthusiasm for teaching courses about which you aren't particularly knowledgeable (e.g., ones you're assigned to teach outside of your specialty) by becoming more knowledgeable about their content. A byproduct of your doing so, incidentally, could be another specialty or a new research interest. I've developed both in this way.

Be Innovative in Your Approaches to Teaching

It's difficult to remain enthusiastic about teaching a course when you teach it almost exactly the same way every time you do so. On the other hand, it's relatively easy to maintain enthusiasm for teaching a course when you're continually modifying it in ways that seem likely to enable you to teach it more effectively.

Form an Informal E-Mail Support Group with Instructors at a Few Other Colleges Who Teach One or More of the Courses That You Teach

Informally exchanging information with others who teach a particular course about approaches for teaching the concepts and/or skills dealt within it more effectively can help you to remain enthusiastic about teaching it. Doing so can also provide you with "sympathetic ears" for airing your frustrations about teaching the course.

Do Research on Aspects of Teaching One or More of the Courses You Teach

A possible source of subject matter for convention presentations, publications, and extramural funding could be developing innovative approaches for teaching certain of the concepts and skills you deal with in your courses. Your classroom would be a laboratory as well as a site for learning. Doing this could not only help you maintain your enthusiasm for teaching, it could also help you meet the publication requirement for tenure and possibly even that for grantsmanship.

Create Print or Electronic Text Material for One or More of Your Courses

I've been a Simon and Schuster college textbook author for more than 25 years. And I've authored texts for all six of the courses I teach. Doing so has enabled me to supplement my income and, perhaps more importantly, maintain my enthusiasm for teaching.

Create a Website for One or More of Your Courses

If you enjoy (or think that you might enjoy) creating and maintaining Internet websites, you might want to consider this possibility. The enjoyment that you would derive from doing so would be likely to help you maintain your enthusiasm for teaching. There is information about possible content for such a website in Chapter 4.

Use Positive Reinforcement to Increase Students' Enthusiasm

As I've indicated previously, your enthusiasm while teaching a class is likely to be affected by the enthusiasm you perceive your students having for how you're teaching it. Consequently, you may be able to increase your enthusiasm by increasing theirs. On way to do this is to positively reinforce behaviors they exhibit that indicate the presence of enthusiasm, such as asking questions and contributing to class discussions.

Develop a New Course and/or Teach Other Existing Ones

You're likely to become bored with teaching if you teach the same courses every semester or every year. One way to cope with such boredom would be to teach different courses. While you're unlikely to be able to completely change your teaching responsibilities, you may be able to develop a new course or trade one with another faculty member. A little of the enthusiasm you gain for teaching by doing so may carry over to your other courses.

Don't Read Student Commentaries About Your Teaching Immediately Before Teaching

If your feelings are hurt easily or you become angered easily by criticism, you'd be wise not to read student commentaries about your teaching immediately before entering a classroom. Even if almost all the comments about your teaching in them are positive, you're likely to remember and be affected by the few that aren't, regardless of whether you feel they're justified. Of course, it would be difficult to be enthusiastic about teaching under such a circumstance. Perhaps it would make most sense to read them when you'd have at least a few days to cope with the negative feelings they elicit before again having to enter a classroom.

Take a Sabbatical or Seek a New Position

These options for coping with a lack of enthusiasm for teaching are more extreme than those mentioned previously. They would be considered last resorts by many academics. Some, of course, don't care very much about how well they teach so they'd be unlikely to consider either of these options to improve their teaching, though they might to strengthen their reputations as scholars.

10

Creating an Environment Conducive to Learning

Students teach themselves and our obligation is to provide an environment that can facilitate their doing so—one that is conducive to learning and extends beyond the classroom. In this chapter we will consider some of the characteristics of such an environment as well as some of the ways that each can be created, facilitated, and/or augmented. The order in which the characteristics are dealt with is mostly an arbitrary one and, consequently, doesn't necessarily indicate the amount that each impacts on learning.

STUDENTS BELIEVE THAT THE TEACHER IS A FAIR, WARM, AND CARING PERSON

Many of the students we interviewed mentioned that it's difficult for them to learn when they have a teacher whom they don't regard as being fair, warm, and caring. A few of them, in fact, commented that one of the most valuable things they learned from a particular teacher was the importance of being fair, warm, and/or caring in professional interpersonal relationships.

If you are a person who is fair, warm and caring, you'll obviously want to communicate being so to your students. You do this by interacting with them, both inside and outside of the classroom, in ways that are likely to convey this message. There are a number of do's and don'ts for doing so in Chapters 12 and 15.

POSITIVE REINFORCEMENT IS USED FAR MORE OFTEN THAN PUNISHMENT

For establishing an environment conducive to learning, positive reinforcement would translate into encouragement and punishment into discouragement. The former tends to enhance prospects for learning and the latter to lessen them.

There are two kinds of errors you can make with regard to encouraging students to strive for goals. You can encourage them to strive for goals that they're incapable of achieving and you can discourage them from striving for goals that they are capable of achieving. While I prefer to avoid both errors, I'd rather make the former than the latter. Consequently, I'm likely to encourage a student to strive to achieve a goal unless it's almost certain that he or she lacks the ability to do so. Ambition is a terrible thing to waste!

On May 20, 2000, I attended our graduation ceremony. Our commencement speaker had been a student in my research design course about 25 years ago. She was not a person whom either I or my colleagues regarded at that time as having a great deal of potential for doing research, but I encouraged her anyway. In her talk she mentioned that she has been employed as a researcher for a number of years and that my encouragement had been a factor in her decision to pursue this vocation. While there undoubtedly have been many such instances when my encouragement had no effect, occasional outcomes such as this one inspire me to continue encouraging rather than discouraging students when it's uncertain whether encouragement is warranted.

THE LEVELS OF STIMULATION USED ARE APPROPRIATE

Students are unlikely to be motivated to learn unless they find doing so stimulating. The manner in which a teacher presents material and otherwise interacts with students can impact significantly on the likelihood they will be adequately stimulated to learn particular material. A student, for example, whom a teacher stimulates to the point of becoming excited about a particular concept, activity, or event is more likely to learn more about it than one who isn't so stimulated.

The level of stimulation that's optimal for learning is neither too much nor too little. While it's fairly obvious why too little stimulation can adversely affect learning, this isn't necessarily the case for too much. The following example may help to clarify why too much stimulation can be detrimental to learning. Boldfacing, italicizing, and setting words and phrases in upper case type are devices textbook authors use to stimulate students to pay particular attention to certain information. If they're overused (e.g., several times on every page), however, their effectiveness as stimulators is likely to diminish. Likewise, emphasizing everything while lecturing is likely to result in students becoming confused and losing the forest for the trees.

STUDENTS FEEL VALUED AND RESPECTED

One characteristic of an environment that's conducive to learning is that students believe they are valued and respected by their teacher. They do not feel that he or she regards them merely as entries in a course grade book. To the contrary, they feel that he or she views them as partners in the learning process—persons with whom it is both possible and rewarding to dialogue and share knowledge.

One way to convey to students that you value and respect them is to encourage them to express their opinions, particularly those that differ from yours, and listen respectfully when they do so. Doing so, incidentally, can help you refine your own opinions. I've benefited tremendously during the past 30 years from encouraging students (even freshmen) to question my points of view.

On the other hand, one way to convey to students that you really don't respect them is to treat them like you would young children or persons whom you don't regard as being very intelligent. An example would be talking down to them. This unfortunately happens quite often when persons who receive their terminal degree from a university that they consider to be "major league" teach at a college or university they consider to be "minor league." That is, they tend to regard many (perhaps most) of their students as inferior to those at their alma mater and they treat them accordingly.

STUDENTS' ANXIETY LEVELS ARE RELATIVELY LOW

It's neither desirable nor possible for a learning environment to be completely anxiety free. A little anxiety about the consequences of not paying adequate attention or otherwise failing to do what the teacher asks can facilitate learning. However, if students' anxiety levels are relatively high, it can hinder rather than facilitate learning. It can also result in students' test grades not adequately reflecting what they've learned. I have at least one student almost every semester who experiences test anxiety to the point that his or her test grades underestimate considerably the amount that he or she has learned. Such test grades obviously aren't reliable indices of learning. Consequently, I take this into consideration when giving final grades to such students, assuming, of course, that I'm aware anxiety was at least partially responsible for their relatively poor test performance.

STUDENTS' ENTHUSIASM LEVELS ARE RELATIVELY HIGH

A necessary condition for an environment being conducive to learning is that both the teacher and students have enthusiasm for learning. If one lacks it, the other is likely sooner or later to do so also.

The level of enthusiasm that both you and your students have for a course is almost certain to affect both how much they learn and how pleasant the course will be for you to teach. The reasons and a number of strategies for enhancing students' enthusiasm for learning are presented in Chapter 9.

STUDENTS ARE ENCOURAGED TO ADHERE TO THE SCIENTIFIC METHOD TO THE EXTENT IT IS POSSIBLE TO DO SO

Regardless of the field a student is preparing to enter, he or she will be expected to know how to evaluate information. Consequently, it is desirable that skills for doing so be reinforced in all the courses a student takes, not just those in his or her major. In other words, it is desirable that the acquisition of discipline-specific content and/or skills not be the only goal for a course. Reinforcing the ability to evaluate information should be one also.

The scientific method contains a set of rules for evaluating the validity, reliability, and generality of information that, if followed, should maximize the likelihood of doing so accurately. One such rule states that all facts, conclusions, and answers to questions should be regarded as tentative and subject to change whenever new information becomes available. This aspect of evaluating information can be reinforced in any course, at least a little.

STUDENTS' SKILLS FOR ACQUIRING AND EVALUATING INFORMATION ARE REINFORCED

As I indicated at the beginning of this chapter, students teach themselves and our obligation is to provide an environment that facilitates their learning to do so efficiently. Ideally, skills for acquiring and evaluating information would be developed and reinforced in such an environment because students need them to teach themselves. Such skills can be reinforced (strengthened) in almost any course.

NECESSARY TOOLS AND EXPERIENCES ARE PROVIDED

In an environment that's conducive to learning, students are provided with the tools and experiences that they need to learn what they're expected to learn. The ones that are optimal for them may not be the ones with which we were provided in a similar course when we were students. There can be several reasons. First, we may not have been provided with the ones available that were optimal for us. That is, the tools and/or experiences we were provided may not have been the best that could have been provided. They could merely have been ones with which our teachers had been provided by their teachers. Just as parents tend to discipline their children the ways their parents disciplined them, people tend to teach like they were taught. Consequently, poor teaching tends to breed poor teaching!

A second reason why the ones that are optimal for them may not be those with which we were provided is that there are technologies available now that weren't available when we were students. There were, for example, no desktop or laptop computers when I was a student nor was there an Internet. The availability and user friendliness of such computers and the Internet make possible learning experiences that would be impossible or impractical without them.

A third reason why the ones that are optimal for them may not be those with which we were provided is that research on teaching the types of material/skills we're teaching may have yielded better ways of doing it since we were students. Some such research is likely to have dealt with the use of new technologies (e.g., interactive multimedia CD-ROM-based instructional material, the Internet, and/or virtual reality).

STUDENT INVOLVEMENT ISN'T ALMOST ALL PASSIVE

Students, whenever possible, should be given opportunities to do rather than just listen (e.g., lectures) and/or watch (e.g., videotapes). This can be done by asking them to discuss or answer questions about what they heard and/or saw. It can also be done by asking them to simulate something about which they are learning. For example, to convey to our students (who are majoring in speech pathology) how people tend to treat you differently if you have a speech disorder, I require them to simulate one in at least three situations outside of the classroom. I've been giving this assignment for more than 25 years, and the ways that the students report being reacted to while simulating are identical to how people tend to react to persons who actually have a speech disorder. No amount of lecturing could convey as well how it feels to have people react to you in these ways.

STUDENTS ARE ENCOURAGED TO PURSUE THEIR INTERESTS

To me, one of the most exciting things that can happen to a teacher is for a student to be sufficiently turned on by something he or she taught to want to pursue it further in spite of the fact that doing so is unlikely to affect his or her course grade. In a student-teacher relationship that's conducive to learning, students are encouraged to pursue such interests. They're also encouraged to pursue course-related interests from sources other than their teacher. Such interests could include research ones that aren't in a niche in which their teacher has (or is attempting to establish) a reputation as a scholar (see Chapter 18).

STUDENTS ARE ENCOURAGED TO PURSUE THEIR "TRUTH," EVEN WHEN IT DIFFERS FROM THAT OF THEIR TEACHER

In an environment that's conducive to learning, students are encouraged to continue seeking the "truth," even when it's likely that what they believe it to be will differ significantly from what their teacher believes it to be. While almost all teachers want their students to accept their truths, they recognize that some of them are unlikely to do so, at least right away. The reason could be a lack of knowledge and/or experience or it could be a strong belief that their truth is more viable (i.e., more strongly supported by data) than that of their teacher. While it can be threatening to have to change the way one views something, it's important for a teacher to be open to doing so and not communicate the message to students, directly or indirectly, that he or she is unwilling "to be confused by facts." And as I've indicated elsewhere in this chapter, accepting the dictum of the scientific method to regard all truths as tentative makes it easier to reject them when new evidence makes it necessary to do so.

STUDENTS ARE ENCOURAGED TO LEARN RATHER THAN JUST DO WELL ON EXAMINATIONS

It's possible for students to do well on an examination without learning very much. And to make matters even worse, much of the information they cram for an examination is unlikely to stay with them very long.

In an environment that's conducive to learning, good grades on examinations are viewed as confirmation of learning rather than ends in themselves. The focus is on acquiring knowledge and skills rather than on doing well on examinations. If students acquire the knowledge and skills they're expected to acquire in ways that are likely to result in their retaining them (i.e., not by cramming), they should get good grades on examinations, assuming, of course, that they don't have text anxiety at a level sufficient to interfere with their doing so.

STUDENTS' ATTEMPTS TO TEACH THEMSELVES ARE REWARDED

Since our ultimate goal should be to provide students with the knowledge, skills, and confidence they need to teach themselves, we should regard their attempts to do so as evidence of progress toward achieving this goal and reward them. That is, we should reinforce their attempts to become independent of us and we should feel good about their doing so. While it certainly would be desirable for teachers to feel this way, the reality is that their attitude toward this occurring is likely to be ambivalent. They're likely to feel that they are less important to their students because they need them less. This is similar to how a parent feels as a child ages and becomes more independent. On the one hand, they are pleased by signs of independence. But on the other hand, it results in their sustaining a loss for which they will have to grieve. That is, both the child becoming independent of the parent and the student becoming independent of the teacher are losses that trigger the grieving process. Since grieving is not particularly pleasant, it's human for teachers, consciously or unconsciously, to do things to sabotage their students becoming independent of them. Their doing so obviously doesn't help to create an environment that is conducive to learning.

STUDENTS' FEELING OF COMPETENCE ARE INCREASED OR AFFIRMED

Teachers, like others, may view the proverbial cup as either half full or half empty. And also like others, they may or may not be perfectionistic. Students who are taught by someone who is neither pessimistic nor perfectionistic are more likely to have their feelings of competence increased or affirmed than they are if taught by someone who is pessimistic or perfectionistic, or worse yet, both.

STUDENTS BELIEVE THAT IT'S POSSIBLE FOR THEM TO BE SUCCESSFUL

Nothing succeeds like success nor fails like failure! The best way to get students to believe that they're capable of learning particular skills or concepts (e.g., computer programming ones) is to create opportunities for them to experience success doing so. It isn't a particularly good idea to initially ask them to do more than they're almost certain to be capable of doing successfully. The certainty of success they're likely to gain in this way can help to sustain their motivation to struggle to get to the next level and that gained there, to higher levels. Initial failure, on the other hand, is likely to reinforce their certainty that they're incapable of learning the skills and/or concepts that they're being expected to learn. Such a certainty is likely to keep them from struggling to learn and, consequently, will increase the likelihood of their failing to do so. This scenario, of course, is one for a self-fulfilling prophecy.

THE INSTRUCTOR SERVES AS A ROLE MODEL FOR TEACHING EFFECTIVELY

How you teach is likely to affect not only your students, but your students' students as well. That is, your students are likely to teach their students at least some of the ways you taught them. Consequently, by teaching well you can benefit not only your students but future generations of students as well. And conversely, by not investing very much in teaching you're likely to harm future generations of students as well as your own.

THE INSTRUCTOR SERVES AS A ROLE MODEL FOR SOMEONE WHO IS AN ENTHUSIASTIC SELF-LEARNER

You're likely to serve as a role model for students when they observe you outside of the classroom as well as within it. If they observe you in your office or laboratory increasing your knowledge and enjoying doing so, they're likely to get the message that learning is a never-ending process that can be enjoyable. On the other hand, if most of the time when they come to (or pass by) your office they observe you gossiping or playing videogames on your computer, they're likely to get a different message, particularly if they rarely (if ever) observe you doing things to increase your knowledge.

11

Making Course Workload Demands Appropriate and Realistic

Almost all course rating forms contain at least one item that taps students' perceptions about whether the workload demands were appropriate and realistic. Their perceptions of one or both may differ from those of the instructor. That is, the instructor may view the workload as having been appropriate and realistic and the students may not. While the instructor may be right, the reality is that the students do the ratings. Consequently, if you want to maximize your ratings, it's crucial to get as many students as possible to perceive your workload demands as having been appropriate and realistic—assuming, of course, that they were. And if they aren't appropriate and realistic, you should modify them to make them so.

Our primary focus in this chapter will be on strategies for maximizing the likelihood that students will perceive your workload demands as both appropriate and realistic. We will begin by looking at what constitutes an appropriate and realistic workload for a course. We will then consider some criteria for determining whether a workload is, in fact, appropriate and realistic. Next, some factors are discussed that can affect students' perceptions of whether a workload is appropriate and realistic. Finally, several strategies are described for getting students to perceive the workload for a course as being both.

WHAT CONSTITUTES AN APPROPRIATE AND REALISTIC WORKLOAD?

A workload that demands too little can be as inappropriate as one that demands too much. While inappropriate workload demands may not discourage students from taking a course, they're highly likely to result in their rating the teaching lower than they would otherwise. If the workload demands are excessive, they may do so out of anger. And if the workload demands are too little, they may do so because they expected to learn more.

Furthermore, a workload that's appropriate and realistic under some circumstances may be appropriate, but unrealistic, under others. The workload that's appropriate and realistic for a course when it's taught during the academic year, for example, may be unrealistic when it's taught during a summer session, or vice versa.

An appropriate workload demand for a course is one that will enable most (but, hopefully, all) of the students to achieve the goals that were established for it. The greater the number of goals and the more difficult they are to achieve, the heavier is likely to be an appropriate workload.

A realistic workload demand for a course is one that most (but, hopefully, all) of the students will be able to meet if they're motivated to do so. Unfortunately, students have only a finite amount of time and energy and there are demands placed on both from sources other than your course (e.g., from the other courses they're taking). Therefore, while the workload demands for a course may be appropriate for achieving course goals, they may be too heavy to be realistic and, consequently, inappropriate. Thus, the workload demands for a course can be inappropriate because they aren't what's needed to achieve course goals, or they're unrealistic because of being too heavy, or both.

If an appropriate workload is too heavy to be realistic, it's crucial that something be done to make it realistic. Possibilities include modifying course goals, finding more efficient (i.e., less time-consuming) ways to achieve course goals, or both.

The fact that a workload is appropriate for the goals of a course and doable doesn't guarantee that students won't find fault with it. They may, for example, regard it as too light because the goals for the course are too few. That is, they may feel that they're getting neither what they need nor their money's worth from the course.

What then is an appropriate and realistic workload for a course? I believe that it's one that's appropriate for the goals of the course and isn't either too heavy to be doable nor too light to provide students with both what they need and adequate value for their tuition.

CRITERIA FOR DETERMINING WHETHER THE WORKLOAD DEMANDS FOR A COURSE ARE APPROPRIATE AND REALISTIC

There are a number of factors to consider when establishing workload demands for a course, if they are to be both appropriate and realistic, including the following:

- The goals.
- What the students will have to do to achieve the goals.
- What you will have to do to achieve the goals.
- Other demands on the students' time and energy.
- The number of weeks the course lasts.
- The number of semester (quarter) hours for which the course is offered.
- The college's regulations regarding the number of hours students are expected to spend outside of class for every hour in class.
- The workload specified in the course syllabus.
- The level of the students.
- The motivation of the students.
- The nature of the workload.

Some implications of each for defining a workload that is both appropriate and realistic will be considered in this section.

The Goals

All courses have goals. An appropriate workload for a course would be one that would, at least theoretically, enable students to attain the goals established for it.

Having too few or too many goals for a course can result in a workload that is inappropriate, unrealistic, or both. Having too many can result in a workload that's unrealistic because of its being too heavy. And having too few can result in a workload that's inappropriate because it isn't meeting students' needs and/or providing adequate value for the tuition they're paying for the course. The latter is particularly likely to be an issue with graduate students, especially older ones.

If attaining the goals established for a course would result in a workload that's either too heavy or too light, there are at least three ways that you may be able to make it more realistic. The first would be to reduce or increase the number of goals. The second would be to increase or reduce the number of semester (quarter) hours for which the course is offered. And the third would be to find more efficient (i.e., less time/energy-consuming) ways to achieve some or all of the goals. The latter is dealt with in the next section.

What the Students Will Have to Do to Achieve the Goals

The workload demands for a course may be appropriate but unrealistic because of other demands being made on the students' time and energy. If a workload is appropriate but unrealistic, there are at least two ways you may be able to modify it to make it realistic. The first would be to eliminate aspects of the workload that aren't essential for achieving course goals. The second would be to substitute tasks that are as appropriate for achieving course goals as the existing ones, but less time- and/or energy-consuming than them.

For each assignment that you're considering, you should ask yourself the following questions:

• For what course goal(s) is this assignment essential?
• How do I know that the assignment will facilitate achieving the goal that I'm using it to facilitate achieving? That is, how do I know that the assignment possesses adequate levels of both validity and reliability for the purpose?
• Is there a less time/energy-consuming alternative that's as appropriate?

Your answers to them should indicate whether the assignment is likely to be of sufficient value to warrant its inclusion in the workload for the course.

What You Will Have to Do to Achieve the Goals

An assignment may be appropriate but unrealistic because of the other demands that are made on your time and energy. These arise from both job-related responsibilities (e.g., research, grant-writing, and student-advising) and personal ones. It may not be practical, for example, for you to assign a particular project because of the amount of time you would have to spend supervising and/or evaluating (grading) it.

Other Demands on the Students' Time and Energy

Your students' other responsibilities have to be considered if you want your workload demands to be both appropriate and realistic. They would tend to be different for married students than for single ones. And they would tend to be different for students who have a job than for full-time ones. If the majority of the students in a course are likely to have many other responsibilities, you'll have to take this into consideration when planning the workload for the course if you want it to be realistic as well as appropriate.

The Number of Weeks the Course Lasts

Certain assignments are more practical when the classes for a course are spread over a semester than when they are taught during a six-week or shorter period (e.g., an intensive summer session or intersession course). And others are more practical when the classes for a course are taught during a period shorter than a semester. Consequently, if you teach a course during both the academic year and summer session, the workloads may have to be different if they are to be realistic.

The Number of Semester (Quarter) Hours for Which the Course Is Offered

The greater the number of semester (quarter) hours for which a course is offered, the heavier you can make the workload without becoming unrealistic.

The College's Regulations Regarding the Number of Hours Students Are Expected to Spend Outside of Class for Every Hour in Class

The greater the number of hours that students are expected to spend outside of class for every hour in class, the heavier you can *theoretically* make the workload without becoming unrealistic. The reality is, however, that many (perhaps most) students don't spend as much time outside of class as such regulations require them to. Other demands on their time can make doing so extremely difficult. Consequently, a workload that appears to be realistic because it is consistent with the institution's regulations may not be so.

The Workload Specified in the Course Syllabus

The workload demands for a course should be specified completely and unambiguously in the syllabus. Students need this information to determine whether they are realistic (considering their other commitments) for when they're planning to take the course. If they aren't realistic, they may be able to delay taking the course or, if it's an elective, substitute another for it.

The Level of the Students

Both the students' level(s) within the college (e.g., juniors) and their intellectual levels are relevant when establishing the workload for a course. A workload that would be unrealistically heavy for a freshman may not be so for a graduate student. And a workload that would be realistic for a course in which almost all of the students are exceptionally bright may not be realistic for one in which only a few of them are so.

The Motivation of the Students

The more willing the majority of the students in a course would be to make completing its workload a priority, the heavier its workload can be before becoming unrealistic. Students in my field (i.e., speech-language pathology), for example, would probably be more willing to make the workload for a practical course in their major a priority than they would that for an elective in their liberal arts core.

The Nature of the Workload

Students enjoy some activities more than others. A workload for a course that consists mostly of activities that students tend to enjoy can be heavier without becoming unrealistic than one that contains few such activities. It, of course, isn't always possible to make such a workload enjoyable.

FACTORS THAT CAN AFFECT STUDENTS' PERCEPTIONS OF WHETHER THE WORKLOAD FOR A COURSE IS APPROPRIATE AND REALISTIC

You can make the workloads for your courses both appropriate and realistic, but if your students don't perceive them as such, they're likely to give you lower teaching ratings than otherwise. There are a number of factors that can affect a student's judgment of whether the workload for a course is appropriate and realistic. Some (perhaps the most important) of these are dealt with in this section. The order in which they're discussed is not intended to indicate the degree to which they affect such judgments.

What the Student Is Expected to Do

The nature of the workload for a course obviously affects the likelihood that it will be perceived as appropriate and realistic. If a student understands how each component of the workload facilitates achieving the goals for the course, he or she is likely to perceive the workload as appropriate, but not necessarily realistic. Some of the factors that can influence a student's perception of the latter are considered elsewhere in this section.

The Student's Expectations for What Constitutes an Appropriate and Realistic Workload

A student is likely to have some sort of expectation for what constitutes a realistic, and possibly even an appropriate, workload for a course. It would, undoubtedly, be based in part on the workloads of similar courses that he or she has had, particularly ones in which he or she did well. This expectation would tend to influence whether he or she perceived the workload for a particular course as being unrealistically heavy, light, or about right.

One aspect of a course workload about which students are particularly likely to have expectations is the amount it is realistic to expect them to read, particularly for material that isn't discussed in class. Some students expect a teacher to discuss all of the material they're expected to read, even if it is material (e.g., a textbook) that the teacher authored and should be relatively easy for them to understand. There could be at least two reasons. First, they may expect to be able to avoid having to read assigned material by relying on what is said about it in class. And second, they may resent being expected to teach themselves. That is, they may believe that their tuition entitles them to be taught.

I've authored the textbooks for the courses I teach, and in class I attempt to go beyond them. From my perspective, I'm giving my students greater value for their tuition than I would if I spent time in class discussing parts of the textbook they can easily understand. However, I've occasionally had students become furious with me because I didn't meet their expectations for how reading assignments should be handled. They apparently felt that I wasn't giving them adequate value for their tuition by expecting them to learn such material on their own. It's crucial, therefore, if you're requiring students to teach themselves (particularly if it's a considerable amount of material) that you communicate to them why you're doing this, particularly if they may not have been expected to do so in the past. This should reduce the likelihood, at least a little, that your teaching ratings will be affected adversely by your requiring them to teach themselves in this way.

Attitudes of Other Students Toward the Workload

A student's perception of whether a course workload is appropriate and realistic is likely to be influenced, at least a little, by that of his or her classmates. If a student's classmates judge a course workload to be inappropriate and/or unrealistic and indicate that they're going to give the teacher lower ratings for this reason than they would have otherwise, he or she is likely to also. Consequently, it's crucial to get at least the majority of your students to perceive your course workloads as being both appropriate and realistic.

The Student's Level of Interest in the Course

The higher a student's level of interest in a course, the more likely he or she is to make its workload a priority and, consequently, the less likely he or she is to perceive it as being too heavy. Since the level of interest that students have in courses in their major tends to be higher than that in others, it's usually possible to make the workload for such courses a little heavier without triggering a judgment that it is unrealistically heavy.

The Workload Demands of the Other Courses That a Student Is Taking

The heavier the workloads for the other courses a student is taking concurrently with yours, the greater the likelihood that he or she will view the workload for yours as excessive. Perhaps your best protection against a student doing so is convincing him or her that the various tasks you assign are both essential and appropriate for achieving course goals.

The Lowest Final Course Grade the Student Considers Acceptable

The lower the final grade that a student regards as acceptable for a particular course, the more likely he or she is to consider its workload excessive. This is particularly true for highly intelligent students who have no interest in a course and are only seeking a passing grade.

The Degree to Which the Various Components of the Workload Affect the Student's Grade

Students are less likely to consider a course's workload demands excessive if they view them as doable and believe that they significantly affect their final course grade. They're particularly likely to complain about time-consuming tasks that have little impact on their course grade if they don't understand why doing them is necessary to achieve course goals.

The Amount of Input That the Student Has Had in Defining the Workload

The more input students have in defining their workload for a course, the less likely they are to regard it as being inappropriate or unrealistic. One way to provide an opportunity for such input is to specify in the syllabus the minimum workload requirements for the various passing final course grades and allow each student to select the grade for which he or she wants to be eligible. A student who is working for an "A" could have an exceptionally heavy workload compared to one who is working for an "C," but it would be by choice. I suspect that few students would choose to work for "Cs," particularly for courses in their major.

STRATEGIES FOR GETTING STUDENTS TO PERCEIVE A WORKLOAD AS BEING APPROPRIATE AND REALISTIC

A number of strategies have been suggested (directly or indirectly) elsewhere in this chapter for getting students to perceive a workload as being both appropriate and realistic. They including the following:

- Requiring students to only do tasks outside of class that are both essential and appropriate for achieving course goals.

- Communicating to students why each assigned task is both essential and appropriate for achieving at least one course goal.

- Keeping the time commitment required to do reading and other assignments realistic.

- Making assignments interesting for students, whenever it's possible to do so.

- Allowing students to choose the passing grade for which they want to be eligible and, thereby, their workload for the course.

- Increasing or reducing the number of semester (quarter) hours for which a course is offered if it is inappropriate for its workload.

While these aren't the only possible strategies for getting students to perceive a course workload as being both appropriate and realistic, they are ones that can be effective for doing so.

12

Establishing an Examination and Grading Policy That Students Are Likely to Consider Fair

While it's highly unlikely that you'll be able to establish an examination and grading policy that all of your students will consider completely fair, you should be able to establish one that most of your students will regard as being adequately fair. It's crucial to do so because one of the most frequent reasons why students give an instructor relatively low teaching ratings is that they consider his or her examination and/or grading policy unfair.

Our focus in this chapter will be on testing and grading. We will begin by considering some possible reasons for giving examinations. Next, the essential components of an examination and grading policy will be delineated along with some criteria for judging its fairness. Following this, some factors will be considered that affect students' judgments about the fairness of an examination and grading policy. And finally, some strategies will be suggested for maximizing the likelihood that students will perceive an examination and grading policy as being adequately fair.

REASONS FOR GIVING EXAMINATIONS

Why give an examination? There are a number of possible answers to this question, four of which are dealt with in this section. The order in which they're considered isn't intended to suggest anything about their relevance for answering this question.

Meeting a Contractual Obligation

Your contractual obligation to your college or university requires you to give each student in each course you teach a grade. The grades you give your students are likely to have to be based, at least in part, on their performance (grades) on examinations. Consequently, to meet this contractual obligation you'll probably have to give examinations whether or not you believe it's meaningful to do so.

On what grounds might the meaningfulness of examinations be questioned? One possibility is the validity and reliability of the grades they yield. They may not indicate sufficiently accurately a student's actual level of knowledge or skill. The reason could be related to the performance of the student, the nature of the examination, or both of these.

How students prepare for and perform while taking an examination can cause their grade to be either lower or higher than it should be, considering the amount they've actually learned and are likely to retain. It could be lower if they experience test anxiety. And it could be higher if they gained most of their knowledge by cramming a few days before the examination. Much of what students learn in this way is likely to be forgotten in a month or so.

An examination may not possess sufficiently high levels of validity and reliability to yield grades that accurately reflect students' knowledge and skill levels. Doing well may merely require them to memorize rather than demonstrate an understanding of concepts and/or the ability to apply what was taught. And even if an examination does attempt to test the latter, the items used to do so may yield data that lack an adequate level of validity and reliability for the purpose. Few teachers systematically evaluate the validity and reliability of the data yielded by examinations that they fabricate.

Motivating Students to Learn

Students are more likely to attempt to learn material if they believe that they're going to be tested on it. A question that I'm asked frequently by students is "Will we be tested on _____ in the examination?" If my answer is no and it's material in a book, I'm certain that at least a few of them won't even skim it. And if it's a videotape that I'll be playing in class and my answer is no, it's likely that at least a few of them won't pay attention to or take notes on it.

Ideally, your students will all be sufficiently interested (and, consequently, motivated) to learn what you want them to learn that you won't have to utilize their desire for good grades (or fear of bad ones) to motivate them to do so. The reality is, however, that not all of them are likely to have this level of interest. Consequently, if you want to maximize the likelihood that almost all of them will at least acquire the amount of knowledge you regard as being minimally acceptable, you'll have to use an external motivator. And among the most effective of these are likely to be either the desire to have a relatively high GPA or the fear of having a relatively low one.

Helping Students to Learn by Providing Them with Feedback About How Well They're Doing

Students need feedback on how well they're learning if they're to be able to fine tune their learning strategies to do so more effectively. One possible source of such feedback is their performance on examinations. Examinations when used in this way function as diagnostic instruments. That is, they provide information that can enable students to fine tune their learning strategies assuming, of course, that they're motivated to do so.

Some types of examinations are better suited for this purpose than are others. For a student's performance on an examination to be useful diagnostically, it's necessary to be possible to infer from it what he or she has to do to improve. Essay examinations are likely to yield more of this type of information than are true/false ones.

Helping the Instructor to Teach More Effectively by Providing Feedback About How Well He or She Is Doing

Just as students need feedback to learn how well they're learning, instructors need feedback to learn how well they're teaching. If the examinations that you give students possess adequate levels of validity and reliability, they can yield information that can enable you to teach both your current course and future ones more effectively. For example, if the performance of some students on an examination indicates that they don't really understand a concept you thought they understood, you can attempt to explain it to them again either during class or an office hour (if only a few of them didn't appear to understand it). And if examination results indicate that the way you're teaching a concept isn't clear to most of your students, you can try to find a clearer way to teach it. You can, of course, use future examination results to determine whether your new way of teaching the concept is clearer than your old way of doing so.

COMPONENTS OF AN EXAMINATION AND GRADING POLICY

It will be necessary for you to have an examination and grading policy that's both comprehensive and clear if you want to minimize the number of arguments you'll have with students about grades and win most of those you do have. Your policy should be reproduced in your syllabi, or on your course-related website (if that you have one), or both. Some of the necessary components of such a policy are described in this section.

The Material on Which Students Will Be Examined

The readings and other materials on which students will be tested in each examination should be conveyed as unambiguously as possible. For books, you may want to include both chapter and page numbers. It's also desirable to indicate whether students are responsible for material in the textbook(s) and other readings that you don't go over in class. Furthermore, you should indicate the types of information that will be presented in class they'll be tested on, including lectures by you, class discussions, presentations by guest speakers, and audio-visual presentations. You might also want to specify the approximate numbers of questions that there will be in examinations from each source (e.g., your lectures).

When Examinations Are Scheduled and/or the Amount of Advanced Notice That Will Be Given if the Dates Aren't in the Syllabus

You can reduce the likelihood of angering students by clearly stating the times and dates for all examinations in the syllabus. If it isn't possible to do so, you should indicate the amount of advanced notice they'll be given. You're likely to anger at least some of them if it's less than two weeks.

The Types of Items

Students tend to prepare differently for an essay examination than they do for a multiple choice, true/false, or fill-in-the-blank one. Consequently, it's desirable to indicate the types of items that may (but not necessarily will) be included in each examination. If the types of items in all examinations will be the same, a single statement (either preceding or following the examination schedule) should be sufficient.

You may also want to indicate whether the questions will tap their ability to recall course-related material, or to apply it, or both. It would be particularly important to do this if you were either considering or planning to include questions that require students to apply (not merely recall) what they learned. Not alerting students to this possibility could result in at least some students considering your examination(s) unfair which, in turn, could result in their giving you lower teaching ratings.

The Number of Items

When I ask students prior to an examination whether they have any questions about it, one of the ones they tend to ask most frequently is "How many questions will there be?" I'm not quite sure why they consider this information helpful for preparing for an examination, but some apparently do consider it so. Perhaps having this information somehow helps them cope with test-related anxiety.

The Amount of Time Students Will Be Given to Complete an Examination

It's particularly important that this be stated if it's longer or shorter than a class session. If it's shorter than one and administered at the beginning, students should be told whether they are to remain in their seat when they finish, leave, or leave and return at a certain time.

You're likely to anger students if an examination is too long for them to finish, or finish comfortably, in the time allotted. You're also likely if you do so to underestimate the amount of knowledge that at least some of them have acquired. A student can fail to answer a question or answer it correctly for one or more of the following reasons: not having time to do so, not having time to formulate an adequate answer, and/or not knowing the answer. It isn't safe to assume that the reason is the latter unless it's highly unlikely to be one of the first two.

Whether the Final Examination Will Be Cumulative

Since the final examinations in some courses are cumulative, students should be informed in the syllabus (and/or on the course website if there is one) about whether it is so in your courses.

The Policy on Making Up Missed Examinations

It's crucial to include a statement of your policy about making up missed examinations. If your department, college, or university has a policy about doing so, you may want to briefly summarize it and refer students to where they can get a more detailed statement (e.g., the institution's catalogue). By not doing so, you increase the likelihood of litigation against both you and your institution by a student who received a lower grade than he or she would have otherwise because of failing to take an examination.

If there's a departmental, college, or university policy against allowing students to make-up examinations they've missed—even when there's for a good reason for their not having taken them—you may want to consider having your own policy about this. I usually allow students to make-up examinations they've missed so long as they can document a legitimate reason for having missed them. Otherwise, the grade that they receive for the course tends to underestimate the amount they've actually learned.

The Policy on Retaking Examinations on Which Grades Were Low

If your department, college, or university has a policy statement about this, you'd be wise to briefly summarize it in the syllabus and refer students to it for more detail, particularly if it doesn't support their having this right. This can enable you to deny students' requests to do so without becoming a "bad guy."

That said, a case can be made for allowing students to retake examinations on which they received a low grade. You would, of course, use a different version of the examination for this purpose. By having to study the material again, they're likely to learn and retain more of it than they would have otherwise. If you're willing to agree that a legitimate reason for using grades is to motivate students to learn, then it would be justifiable to use them for this purpose.

The Policy on Extra-Credit Assignments

If you have extra-credit assignments, they should be described in the syllabus and the amount(s) of extra credit that can be earned by doing each should be indicated. An example of such an assignment is volunteering to participate in graduate student or faculty research. Having extra-credit assignments can both encourage and reward students for going beyond the basics.

The Number of Examinations on Which Final Grades Will Be Based

Most students prefer to have their final grade for a course based on more than a mid-semester and final examination. You may want to consider giving at least three examinations in those courses in which there aren't any projects on which students are graded.

The Amount of Input That Students Will Have Regarding the Number and Types of Examinations

Students are more likely to regard the examination policy for a course as fair if they've had some input in defining it. For this reason, some instructors give students choices with regard to the number and types of examinations. If you decide to do this, you may find it expedient to give them a limited number of choices for each (two or three) and have them vote for the ones they want by raising their hands.

The Criteria Used for Grading Examinations

You should indicate both what (if anything) causes points to be deducted other than incorrect information and how grades are determined. An example of something other than incorrect information that could cause points to be deducted is spelling technical terms incorrectly.

With regard to how grades are determined, you should indicate whether they're based on absolute point totals or on a curve. I tend to favor basing them on absolute point totals for two reasons. First, I encourage all of my students to learn enough to earn a high grade. I'd tend to feel very good about my teaching if all of the students in a course learned enough to earn an "A." And second, grades that are based on a curve tend to be less reliable indicators of learning than are those based on absolute point totals. In part, this is because they're influenced not only by what the students to which they're given learned, but also by what the others who took the course the same semester learned. A particular point total that would earn an "A" one semester might earn a "C" the next, or vice versa.

The Feedback Students Will Receive About Their Performance on Examinations

Your statement should indicate whether examinations will be handed back or grades will be posted and when, where, and how it will be done. If you'll be handing back examinations but students won't be allowed to keep them (just look them over), you may want to indicate this.

Your Openness to Allowing Students to Question Grading

Some students will question how you graded their examinations regardless of your openness to having them do so. While you certainly want students to view you as open to correcting mistakes you've make in grading their examinations, you may also want to encourage them to attempt to convince you that some of their answers are correct even though they differ from yours. There should be a sentence or two in the policy statement indicating your willingness to hear such arguments if you want to encourage students to present them.

The Speed at Which Examinations Will Be Graded

Students expect to find out how well they did on an examination a relatively short time after taking it. If you won't be able to provide them with such feedback quickly, you may want to include a statement giving the reason(s) in your syllabus.

Cheating

Your institution undoubtedly has a policy about cheating and students should be referred to it.

Having to deal with an accusation of cheating is likely to be highly uncomfortable for you, your department, and your institution, as well as the student being accused of doing it and his or her family. Consequently, the best way to minimize the likelihood of having to cope with such discomfort is doing whatever you can to prevent cheating. Not seating students close enough to each other to be able to see each others' papers and observing students closely while they're taking an examination are examples of things you can do to reduce opportunities for their doing this.

DETERMINING WHETHER AN EXAMINATION AND GRADING POLICY IS FAIR

Fairness is a judgment rather than a description. Consequently, the examination and grading policy for a course is fair if it is regarded as such by both the instructor and the majority of the students in it.

It's also desirable, incidentally, for an instructor's examination and grading policy to be considered fair by the senior faculty in the instructor's department and by his or her dean. These are the persons to whom students are likely to complain if they consider it unfair. If the dean and the instructor's colleagues also regard it as such, they may be unable "in good conscience" to enthusiastically support the instructor's bid for tenure.

Faculty and administrators agree quite well with each other on a number of the attributes of an examination and grading policy that's fair. Some of those that are relevant for judging the fairness of a test are dealt with in this section. The order in which they're discussed isn't intended to suggest their importance.

How and When Students Are Informed About the Test

This is only likely to become an issue for tests whose dates aren't printed in the syllabus. If test dates are announced in class rather than in the syllabus, all of the students may not be present when they're announced. Also, students may not be given sufficient advanced notice of a test for it to be regarded as fair by them and others. Many persons in academia would consider giving students less than two weeks notice for a test as being unfair.

The Validity of the Items on the Test

The items on a test are valid if students' responses to them provide meaningful information about how close they are to achieving one or more course goals. If, for example, a course goal was to have students acquire an understanding of a certain terminology, then test items that provided meaningful information about how well they understood it (e.g., required them to define terms that are a part of it) would be valid.

The Length of the Test

If a test is too long for almost all of the students to have time to finish and it isn't intended to assess the ability to perform certain tasks rapidly, then a case can be made for it being invalid and possibly also unfair. Some students take longer than others to respond to test items. There could be a number of reasons, including anxiety. Consequently, if your goal is to determine the amount of information that students have acquired, it will be difficult for you to do this if a test is too long to allow almost all of them to finish because the reason for questions not being answered—or being answered superficially—could be insufficient time, insufficient knowledge, or both.

The Appropriateness of the Test for the Particular Students to Whom It Is Administered

If a test is to be both fair and effective for motivating and rewarding students for learning, it must not be excessively challenging to do well on it. A type of test that would be excessively challenging for a freshman to do well on may not be so for a doctoral student. And a test that would be excessively challenging for most of the students in a particular course at a small state university to do well on may not be so for most of those in that course at an "Ivy League" one.

The Appropriateness of How the Test Is Administered

While how a test is administered isn't one of the main reasons for one being considered unfair, it can result in such a judgment. If, for example, an instructor arrived late to a test session and didn't give the students extra time to complete the test, his or her failure to do so could be considered unfair.

The Reliability and Objectivity of the Method Used to Score Test Items

A scoring scheme that's highly subjective is unlikely to yield reliable data (grades) and it's failure to do so can, with some justification, be considered unfair. This is far more likely to be a concern when scoring essay questions than when scoring multiple-choice ones. Perhaps the only fairness-related concern for scoring multiple-choice questions is the presence of answers other than the ones the instructor considers correct that can also be regarded as correct. This is particularly likely to be a concern when more than one foil is at least partially correct and the student is asked to select the one that's most correct. The foil that the instructor considers the most correct may not be the only one that can be viewed as being so.

The Method Used to Translate Scores into Grades

This is most likely to raise fairness-related questions if the use of a curve results in many students receiving considerably lower grades than they would have otherwise because most of the scores are quite high. While a high percentage of students getting high scores on a test could indicate that there was something wrong with the test, it could also indicate that a high percentage of them were motivated to learn the material on which they were tested. Grading on a curve in such a case could (with some justification) be considered unfair.

The Method Used to Provide Feedback to Students About Their Performance

Fairness regarding such feedback is only likely to be an issue if it is provided in a way that enables students to know, or infer, each others grades. This could happen, for example, if you were to pass back examinations in class in an order that would communicate whether particular students received relatively high or relatively low grades. You could inadvertently do this, for example, by ordering a set of examinations by scores before assigning grades to them and not "shuffling" the set before returning them.

FACTORS THAT AFFECT STUDENTS' JUDGMENTS ABOUT THE FAIRNESS OF AN EXAMINATION AND GRADING POLICY

How students rate the fairness of your examination and grading policy will be determined by how they perceive it, which could differ significantly from how you and your colleagues do so. Consequently, to maximize your teaching ratings you'll have be aware of the factors that can cause students to perceive such a policy as being either fair or unfair. A number of them are dealt with in this section. The order in which they're presented isn't intended to suggest their likelihood of affecting such perceptions.

The Types of Items in an Examination

Students may question the fairness of certain types of test items. One such type is the true/false one. Some students who are very knowledgeable do poorly on such items because they're more aware of exceptions to statements that should be marked "true" than their less-knowledgeable peers.

That said, I believe that well-crafted true/false items can be quite useful for assessing students' understanding of concepts and principles, in part, because they can't be answered by a process of elimination like multiple-choice ones often can.

While students tend to regard the use of multiple-choice items as being fairer than that of true/false ones, there are at least two types of multiple-choice items that many tend to consider unfair. The first is the type for which there may be either more than one correct foil or no correct foils and, consequently, at least one foil which states that several, all, or none of the others are correct. And the second is the type for which there is more than one foil that could be correct and students are asked to select the one that's most correct.

Students may also have some concerns about the fairness of essay items, particularly with regard to how they are scored. If you're unable to maintain a constant standard while scoring such items, the fairness of your scoring is likely to be questioned. One scenario by which this could happen would be two students who gave essentially the same response to an item comparing their responses and finding that the scores they received were quite different.

The Numbers of Items in an Examination

Students may consider an examination unfair because they perceive the number of items in it as being either too few or too many. If they perceive the number as being too few, the reason is likely to be concern about losing too many points for an incorrect answer. And if they perceive it as being too many, the reason is likely to be having insufficient time to respond adequately to all items.

The Number of Examinations Given

Like the number of items in an examination, students may consider the number of examinations unfair because they perceive it as being either too few or too many. If they perceive the number as being too few, the reason is likely to be concern about a relatively low grade on one significantly reducing their final course grade. And if they perceive the number as being too many, the reason is likely to be having to spend more time studying than they consider acceptable.

Their Grades on Examinations

Students tend to question the fairness of any examination for which they feel they prepared adequately and yet received a lower grade than that they anticipated. They're particularly likely to do so if a number of their classmates whom they regard as being good students do also. It isn't necessary for students to receive low grades for them to perceive an examination as being unfair for this reason. A "B+" could do it for a student who usually receives "A's."

The Extent to Which the Examination Covers All of the Material That They Studied

Students are likely to question the fairness of an examination if it doesn't contain items on all of the material they were required to study for it. A good way to anger students is to require them to read some chapters in a book or some papers and not include any items on them in the test.

The Extent to Which Their Grades on Examinations Accurately Reflect the Amount They've Learned

Students who feel that they've learned a great deal are likely to consider an examination to be at least a little unfair if it doesn't allow them to demonstrate the extent of their knowledge, even if the grade they receive is an "A."

The Way That Examination and Course Grades Are Computed

As I've indicated previously, students are likely to consider grading that is done on a curve to be unfair if it results in their receiving a lower grade than they would have otherwise.

STRATEGIES FOR GETTING STUDENTS TO PERCEIVE AN EXAMINATION AND GRADING POLICY AS BEING FAIR

A number of strategies have been suggested (directly or indirectly) elsewhere in this chapter for getting students to perceive an examination and grading policy as being fair. They including the following:

- Communicate to students as unambiguously as possible *at least twice* (e.g., on the syllabus and in class) the list of readings and other materials that will be covered on an examination.
- If it's possible to do so, list the dates for all examinations in the syllabus. And if doing so isn't possible, give students at least two weeks advanced notice for any that aren't listed.
- Inform students about the types of items (e.g., essay questions) that may be on the examination.

- Avoid having too many items (questions) on an examination for students to be able to finish it comfortably.
- Make certain that the items are appropriate (not excessively challenging) for the particular students to whom the examination is given.
- Avoid items that don't provide meaningful information about how close students are to achieving one or more course goals.
- Inform students about the approximate number of items that there'll be on the examination.
- If an examination is administered at the beginning of a class, tell students what they are to do if they finish early (i.e., remain in their seat or leave).
- Indicate in the syllabus whether the final examination will be cumulative.
- Include a statement of your policy about making up missed examinations in the syllabus.
- If you permit students to retake examinations, include a statement about the circumstances under which they're allowed to do so in the syllabus.
- If there are extra-credit assignments, describe them in the syllabus.
- Base final grades on at least three examinations if there are no assignments that contribute significantly to it.
- Give students choices regarding the number of examinations and types of items on them.
- Indicate either in the syllabus, in class, or both what (if anything) causes points to be deducted other than incorrect information and how grades are computed.
- Avoid grading on a curve if doing so results in students receiving lower grades than they would have otherwise.
- Indicate either in the syllabus, in class, or both whether examinations will be handed back or grades will be posted and when, where, and how it will be done.
- Indicate straightforwardly in the syllabus how you prefer to deal with questions concerning (challenges to) grading.
- Indicate your policy about cheating in the syllabus and observe students closely during examinations to reduce their opportunities for doing so.

While these aren't the only possible strategies for maximizing the likelihood that students will perceive a course examination and grading policy as being fair, they are ones that are likely to be effective for doing so.

13

Utilizing Class Time Well

All courses—even those taught by correspondence, the Internet, television, and other forms of distance learning—require a student to spend some time interacting with an instructor (i.e., in class). What an instructor does while doing so and how he or she does it determines whether students will perceive the time they spent interacting with him or her (i.e., in class) as having been utilized well. Their perceptions regarding this are likely to significantly influence the teaching ratings that they give the instructor. Our focus in this chapter will be on how the time spent interacting with students can be utilized so that students are likely to perceive it as having been utilized well.

WHY SHOULD STUDENTS WANT TO SPEND TIME IN CLASS?

If students are to perceive the time they spend in class as being time well spent, they must be aware of the goals that they want attending classes to help them achieve and believe that what transpires while they are there is helpful for achieving them. Goals that should be at least partially achievable by attending classes include the following:

- Meeting institutional, departmental, and instructors' attendance requirements for receiving credit for the course and/or not having the final course grade reduced by exceeding the maximum number of cuts allowed.
- Averting feelings of guilt (arising from cutting classes).
- Acquiring information that isn't dealt with in the textbook(s) and/or assigned readings.

- Gaining a deeper understanding of the concepts that are dealt with in the text-book(s) and/or assigned readings.
- Acquiring or refining skills.
- Benefiting from other students' knowledge and experience.
- Getting to know and be well thought of by the instructor (e.g., for recommendations).
- Pleasure!

There, of course, can be other goals that attending class can help a student to achieve.

WAYS TIME CAN BE SPENT IN A CLASSROOM THAT CAN FACILITATE STUDENTS ACHIEVING THEIR GOALS

There are a number of ways that an instructor can utilize the time he or she spends with students that can (but not necessarily will) result in their perceiving it as having been well spent because it helped them to achieve their goals. Some of these are dealt with in this section. The order in which they're dealt with isn't intended to communicate anything about their desirability or usefulness for this purpose.

Taking Attendance

Students who aren't particularly interested in a course may have to cope with a strong impulse to cut classes. Their doing so will reduce the likelihood that they'll both develop an interest in the course and learn very much. Taking attendance at each class session, therefore, is likely to help at least a few students to cope successfully with this impulse. The amount of class time needed to do so can be kept to less than a minute by passing an attendance sheet.

Lecturing

Lecturing is one of the main ways that instructors utilize class time. The degree to which it's likely to be helpful to students is determined by a number of factors, including the following:

- The relevance of the material.
- The extent to which the material doesn't merely replicate that in the textbook(s) and other required readings.
- The clarity with which the material is communicated.
- The ability of the instructor to hold the students' attention.

Some considerations concerning these are dealt with elsewhere in the chapter.

Asking Relevant Questions

Asking questions can be used in at least two ways to facilitate learning. First, attempting to answer them forces students to become actively involved with what's being taught. Students are more likely to learn skills and understand concepts and principles if their involvement with them is active rather than passive. And second, asking questions gets and holds students' attention (for at least a short while). Doing so can, therefore, be an effective way to regain students' attention when you lose it while lecturing.

Whether time spent in class asking questions is likely to be perceived by students as time well spent will be determined, in part, by the types of questions asked. According to Wlodkowski (1978, p. 98), the questions that instructors ask in class can be of one or more of the following six types:

1. *Knowledge questions*—These usually depend on rote memory and require students to recall or recognize information: "Who invented the automobile?"
2. *Comprehension questions*—These require students to interpret, compare, or explain what they have learned: "Could you explain in your own words the meaning of this definition?"
3. *Application questions*—These require students to use what they have learned to solve problems: "According to our definition of creativity, which of the following behaviors would be considered creative?"
4. *Analysis questions*—These require students to identify causes and motives as well as to infer, deduce, and generalize: "Why do people respond differently to similar frustrations?"
5. *Synthesis questions*—These require students to think divergently (creatively) in solving problems, producing ideas, and developing any kind of intellectual response: "What would an ideal modern city be like to you?"
6. *Evaluation questions*—These require students to judge or appraise anything they are perceiving: "Which president since 1936 has been the most effective?"

Questions of the first type (i.e., knowledge questions) tend to be the least effective for both learning and having students perceive the time spent answering them as time well utilized.

Facilitating Small and Large Group Discussions

Discussions in which students are encouraged to generalize and/or apply concepts and principles can facilitate a deeper understanding of them. They also can provide a way for students to gauge how well they understand them. If the depth of your understanding of a particular concept or principle is inadequate, it's likely to be evident to at least a few of the others with whom you're discussing it and they're likely to communicate this to you verbally, nonverbally, or both.

Using Visual and Audio Aids

Some concepts and principles are difficult to define by words alone. It helps to supplement verbal definitions of them with extensional ones—that is, to present visual and/or auditory images that illustrate them (Johnson, 1946). Presenting objects, videotapes, audiotapes, multimedia CD-ROM disks, and/or other images that clarify them is likely to be perceived by students as time well utilized. However, if it isn't obvious to students why you're using such aids, they're likely to perceive your doing so as merely a way to either fill time or avoid having to lecture and, consequently, not as being time well utilized.

Doing Demonstrations

Demonstrations, like visual and audio aids, are a way to clarify verbal definitions of concepts and principles by supplementing them with extensional ones. And they, also like visual and audio aids, are likely to be perceived by students as being worthwhile if their relevance is obvious to them.

Providing Simulations

Simulations are a type of demonstration in which students are active participants rather than passive observers. As such, they can be used to clarify concepts and principles and are likely to be perceived by students as being worthwhile if they do so. An example would be having students put ear plugs in their ears to experience what it's like to have a conductive hearing loss.

Developing Skills

Laboratory and other types of experiences can be provided that enable students to develop and/or refine particular skills. As long as students are aware of their purpose and the skills are ones that they're motivated to develop or refine, they're likely to perceive the time they spend developing or refining them as time well utilized.

Having Students Do Presentations (i.e., Teach Each Other)

One of the best ways to deepen your understanding of a concept or principle is to attempt to teach it to someone. Consequently, having students do presentations cannot only be helpful to their classmates, but also to themselves. It, of course, is essential that they both understand the concepts or principles they're presenting and present them in a way that's likely to be understandable to their classmates.

Having Guest Speakers and/or Resource Persons

Guest speakers and resource persons (consultants) are likely to be appreciated by students if they deepen their understanding of concepts and/ or principles that they regard as relevant or if they facilitate their acquiring or refining a skill. An example of the latter would be a professional musician conducting a "master's class" for aspiring musicians in which he or she critiques their performance.

Having Field Trips

These—like audiovisual aids, demonstrations, and simulations—can deepen students' understanding of concepts and principles by supplementing verbal definitions with extensional ones. Students are likely to consider the time spent on field trips as well utilized if they're cognizant of their purpose and regard it as relevant.

FACTORS THAT CAN AFFECT STUDENTS' PERCEPTIONS OF HOW WELL THE TIME THAT THEY SPENT WITH THEIR INSTRUCTOR(S) WAS UTILIZED

To maximize the likelihood that students will perceive (and, therefore, rate) the time that they spend with you in the classroom as well utilized, it's crucial that you be cognizant of the factors that can affect their judgments about this. A number of them are dealt with in this section. Most were mentioned by at least a few of the undergraduate and graduate students who were participants in a structured-interview survey done by one of my graduate students (Amy E. Marcum) in April 2000. The order in which they're considered doesn't necessarily reflect the amount that they're likely to affect such judgments.

The Relevance, Importance, and Practicality of the Material Presented

This is the factor that the students in our survey mentioned most frequently. While the relevance, importance, and practicality of the material we're presenting may seem obvious to us, it may not be to at least some of our students. Keep in mind that we know more about the material and its ramifications than do most of our students.

Students tend to pay more attention to material they regard as relevant, important, and practical than they do to that they regard otherwise. Consequently, spending a little time in class documenting the relevance, importance, and practicality (assuming that there is some) of the material you'll be presenting is likely to increase the amount your students learn (and for this reason the likelihood that they'll consider the time they spent with you to have been time well utilized).

The Instructor's Effectiveness as a Lecturer (Communicator)

This is also a factor that was mentioned often by the students in our survey. They indicated that they tend to pay more attention to a lecturer whom they regard as interesting than to one whom they regard as boring regardless of the relevance, importance, and practicality of the material that he or she is presenting. Obviously, the more attention they pay to a lecturer, the more they're likely to learn. And the more they learn, the more likely they are to perceive the time they spent doing so as having been well utilized.

The students in our survey when asked what characteristics lecturers whom they regarded as interesting tended to have, mentioned the following:

- They present material in ways that hold students' interest.
- They're approachable, genuine, and interact with students on a personal level.
- They learn students' names and are available to them outside of the classroom.
- They stay on task (i.e., don't go off on tangents).
- They don't appear to be saying the same thing over and over again.
- They have a wide knowledge base.
- They admit being unsure of an answer when they are.
- Their speech is easy to understand and they explain ideas clearly.
- They allow students to ask questions when needed.
- They appear to be interested in the material about which they're lecturing.
- They have a good sense of humor.
- They have control of the class.

These, of course, are unlikely to be the only characteristics that lecturers whom students perceive as interesting possess.

The Organization of the Material Presented

The more organized the lectures and other class activities, the more likely students are to perceive the time they spend in class as time well spent. For lectures, students tend to judge organization, at least in part, by the ease with which they're able to take meaningful notes. You can, incidentally, make lectures more student-friendly for note taking by using presentation software (e.g., PowerPoint) to summarize the topics on which you'll be lecturing on overhead transparencies or slides and projecting the overhead transparency or slide on which you're lecturing while doing so.

The Examples Used

Students are likely to perceive the time spent on examples that deepen their understanding of concepts or principles as being well utilized. Whether particular examples are perceived in this way is a function of their relevance, their clarity, and their appropriateness for the particular group of students with which they are used. With regard to the latter, an example that's meaningful to a class consisting mostly of middle-aged graduate students may not be so to one consisting mostly of seventeen-year-old freshmen.

The Instructor's Adherence to the Schedule/Outline in the Syllabus

Students tend to perceive class time as not being well utilized if an instructor fails to adhere to the schedule and/or topic outline in the syllabus. With regard to the former, if a session-by-session topic schedule is printed in the syllabus and the instructor fails to adhere to it, at least some students are likely to conclude that the amount of time he or she devoted to some topics was inappropriate (either too much or too little). And if the discussion of individual topics doesn't conform to that in the syllabus, at least some students are likely to question whether class time was well utilized because of the difficulty they're having taking notes and/or because of their concluding that the instructor goes off on tangents (something that students, rightly or wrongly, tend to view as a waste of class time). If in your courses you're unlikely to be able to adhere to a strict class schedule or if the order in which you talk about topics tends to vary a little from semester to semester, you'd be wise to not include a detailed schedule or topic outline in your syllabi.

The Relevance of the Audio and Visual Aids, Field Trips, Demonstrations, Simulations, and Presentations by Guest Speakers/Consultants That Were Utilized

You'd probably be wise to assume that at least some of your students will perceive audio and visual aids, demonstrations, simulations, presentations by guest speakers (or consultants), and field trips as merely being ways for you to fill time unless you establish their relevance. It isn't safe to assume that their relevance will be obvious to students. Your not doing so could result in students paying less attention than that needed to benefit significantly from such presentations.

Whether the Instructor Begins Classes by Asking if There Are Any Questions and Allows Time for Them at the End

Students are likely to regard time spent at the beginnings and ends of classes answering their questions as being well utilized. Even if they have no questions, they appreciate the opportunity to ask them as long as the instructor's desire to be helpful in this way appears to be sincere.

Whether the Instructor Begins Class with an Overview and Ends It with a Summary

A formula for organizing an oral presentation that many speakers find helpful is the following: tell them what you're going to tell them, tell them, and tell them what you told them. The request by some of our interviewees for instructors to begin class with an overview and end it with a summary is consistent with this formula. Both the overview and summary should, of course, be relatively short.

The Willingness of the Instructor to Answer Questions Before Moving on

Students tend to appreciate the opportunity to ask questions when they occur to them and usually don't object to other students doing so as long as their questions are relevant. The down side of allowing students to do this is risking losing your train of thought. You could, of course, delay answering questions for a bit when you're at considerable risk for doing so.

The Extent to Which the Instructor Is Prepared and Up-to-Date in All Needed Areas

Students are likely to consider an instructor whom they perceive as not being adequately prepared or as presenting material they regard as being out of date (old) to be wasting their time. Their perception about the preparedness of an instructor or the appropriateness of the material that he or she presents is influenced by their attitude toward the instructor, as well as by what the instructor actually does. If they believe that an instructor doesn't prepare adequately and/or presents out-of-date material, they're more likely than otherwise to conclude that he or she has done so again. Consequently, if some of the material you'll be presenting isn't of recent origin, it's crucial that you communicate to students prior to presenting it why it's still relevant and/or worth learning.

Whether Classes Usually Begin and End on Time

Instructors who often are either late to class or end classes early are less likely than otherwise to be perceived as utilizing class time well. And instructors who end classes late often are also likely to be rated lower than they would be otherwise because of a time issue (i.e., students having less time than they need to get to where they have to be next).

The Degree to Which Students' Participation Is Active Rather than Passive (e.g., the Amount of Time They Spend Participating in Small Group Discussions or Projects)

Everything else being equal, students are likely to perceive classes in which their participation is active as being more helpful (i.e., as being time better spent) than those in which their participation is passive. There could be at least two reasons. First, they tend to pay more attention in classes in which they're expected to be active participants. And second, doing helps them to learn. It's usually easier, for example, to learn to use a computer program by doing a tutorial than by listening to someone explain how to use it.

Whether the Amount of Material Presented in Each Class During the First Few Weeks of a Course Is Approximately the Same as That Presented During the Last Few Weeks

Some instructors tend to present considerably more material during the last few weeks of a course than they do during the first few. The reason usually is that it took them longer than expected to get through some of the material and, consequently, they have to speed up to get through all of it. Judging by responses from our interviewees, students strongly dislike this happening and perceive it as resulting from the instructor not managing time well. If this happens to you often, perhaps you're not managing time well and/or attempting to present too much information.

The Extent to Which the Instructor Varies Activities to Maintain Student Interest

The more frequently students experience boredom in class, the less strongly they are to perceive the instructor as utilizing time well. Students are more likely to experience boredom if the content of every class is the same than if the instructor varies (at least a little) what transpires. The same can be true for a single class, particularly one that lasts for several hours. A number of activities are described elsewhere in this chapter that can be combined with lecturing to reduce the likelihood of boredom.

The Tendency of the Instructor to Repeat Himself or Herself and/or Go Off on Tangents

All instructors repeat themselves, at least occasionally. And all instructors probably go off on what can be perceived as being tangents, at least occasionally. Just as George Washington and Yasser Arafat could legitimately be perceived by their contemporaries as being either terrorists or freedom fighters, an instructor could be perceived as being a poor teacher because he or she wastes time by repeating things a number of times or as being a good teacher because he or she really wants students to understand and retain certain concepts and principles and realizes that repetition is necessary for them to do so. Likewise, what could be perceived as going off on a tangent could also be perceived as an attempt to deepen students' understanding of a concept or principle. If you're criticized frequently by students for repeating material and/or going off on tangents and your reasons are legitimate, you're likely to find it worthwhile (for ratings, etc.) to communicate your rationale for doing so, preferably at the beginning of each course that you teach.

STRATEGIES FOR MAXIMIZING THE LIKELIHOOD THAT STUDENTS WILL PERCEIVE THE TIME THEY SPEND IN CLASS AS BEING WELL UTILIZED

A number of strategies have been suggested (directly or indirectly) elsewhere in this chapter for getting students to perceive the time that they spend in class as being well utilized. They include the following:

- Communicate the relevance, importance, and practicality of the material you'll be presenting. Don't assume that it will be obvious to your students.
- Strive to lecture in a manner that's likely to hold your students' interest (specifics are detailed elsewhere in this chapter).
- Organize your lectures so that they'll be student-friendly for note taking.
- Use examples that students are likely to consider relevant, clear, and appropriate.
- If you include a session-by-session schedule and/or topic outline in a syllabus, adhere to it.
- Assume that at least some of your students won't perceive the relevance of your audio and visual aids, demonstrations, simulations, presentations by guest speakers (or consultants), and field trips unless you establish it.
- Begin classes by asking if there are any questions and allow time for them at the end.

- At each lecture, begin by telling them what you're going to tell them, tell them, and end by telling them what you told them.
- Whenever possible, answer students' questions before moving on.
- Be adequately prepared and up to date.
- Begin and end classes when they're scheduled to begin and end.
- Whenever possible, have students' participation be active rather than passive.
- Have the amount of material you present in each class during the first few weeks of a course be approximately the same as that you present during the last few weeks.
- Vary activities to maintain student interest.
- If students criticize you frequently for repeating material and/or going off on tangents and your reasons are legitimate, communicate your rationale for doing so.

While these aren't the only possible strategies for maximizing the likelihood that students will perceive the time that they spend in class as being well utilized, they are ones that are likely to be effective for doing so.

14

Being Available and Helpful Outside of Class

Students expect to be able to meet and otherwise communicate with their teachers outside of class. My university requires faculty to be available to students in their office at least six hours a week. If your students don't perceive you as being both readily available and helpful to them outside of class, at least some are likely to give you significantly lower teaching ratings than they would otherwise.

We'll be exploring in this chapter issues related to communicating with students outside of the classroom. We'll begin by delving into how a teacher's attitude toward doing this can affect both his or her teaching ratings and students. We'll then look at options for doing such communicating. Next, we'll consider some of the more common reasons why students seek to do so. And finally, I'll suggest some strategies for maximizing the likelihood of your being perceived by students as available and helpful outside of class.

COMMUNICATING WITH STUDENTS OUTSIDE OF THE CLASSROOM—A NECESSARY EVIL OR BLESSING?

The amount that you're likely to benefit from spending time with students outside of the classroom will be determined, in large part, by your attitude toward doing so. If you view spending time in this way as a necessary evil, you're likely to benefit less from doing so than you are if you view it as a blessing. Consequently, you'd be wise to try to find ways to view it as the latter rather than the former.

If you don't consider spending time in this way a blessing and would like to do so, you may find one or more of the following compelling for convincing yourself that it can be:

- It gives you an opportunity to get to know at least some of your students as people, thereby making it easier, for example, to write recommendations for them.
- It gives you an opportunity to resolve conflicts with students before they're communicated to your chairperson or dean. Frequent complaints about you to them or to other faculty in your department are unlikely to enhance your prospects for being tenured.
- It provides an opportunity to impact positively and significantly on your students' academic and personal lives.
- It provides an opportunity to enhance students' interest in your field and/or mentor students.
- It provides an opportunity to identify students who might be interested in participating in your research or whose research (thesis, dissertation, etc.) you can direct.
- If you teach well, this type of interaction with students is likely to enhance the pleasure you'll derive from teaching. It may even provide you with a few friends. A number of my students during the past 30 years became so after they graduated.

WAYS TO MAKE ONESELF AVAILABLE TO STUDENTS OUTSIDE OF THE CLASSROOM

There are several ways that you can communicate with students outside of the classroom. Most instructors who encourage students to do so use two or more of them. The most common ones are dealt with in this section. The order in which they're discussed isn't intended to convey anything about their usefulness.

Office Hours and "By Appointments"

The face-to-face meeting is the main way that instructors have traditionally made themselves available to students outside of class. They schedule a certain number of hours each week to meet with students and/or make appointments to meet with them at times that are convenient for both the students and themselves. If you have regular office hours, you may want to put a card on your office door listing them and also include them in your syllabi.

Some faculty require students to make appointments to meet with them during their office hours. Others see students on a first-come-first-seen basis. And still others use some combination of these two. Two advantages of requiring all students to make appointments is that you don't have to be in your office during an office hour that no student has made an appointment to see you and students probably won't have to wait near your office for long periods of time to be seen.

One comment that was made repeatedly by the students whom we interviewed was that they disliked instructors who are only available to them during their office hours, particularly if their class and/or work schedule preclude their meeting with them at these times. You'd be wise, therefore, to give students the option of meeting with you "by appointment" at times other than your office hours. While few are likely to utilize this option, the fact that you offer it tends to reinforce their perception of your being available to them.

Telephones, Answering Machines, and Voice Mail

The reason why a student may need your help may not require a face-to-face meeting. A telephone call may be all that's needed. Students are likely to regard it as advantageous if problems can be dealt with in this way because they won't have to wait for an office hour/appointment to talk with you nor will they have to travel to your office. It could also be advantageous to you because it would probably take less of your time than a face-to-face meeting. Telephones, answering machines, and voice mail can, of course, also be used for making appointments and following up on face-to-face meetings.

You may want to give students your home telephone number as well as your office one. Students are particularly likely to appreciate your doing so if you don't spend much time on campus. You'd be wise, however, to check with your spouse and/or others with whom you live before giving it to students. He, she, or they may not want to have to answer and/or cope with calls from them.

Snail Mail, Campus Mail, and Fax

These are useful primarily for exchanging papers and other documents with students. If you have a fax machine (or a computer programmed to simulate one) at home, you may want to give students the number for it.

E-Mail

This has been one of the main ways that I've made myself available to both present and past students during the past few years. I check my e-mail several times a day and usually respond immediately. I include my e-mail address on course syllabi and encourage students to initially contact me in this way about a problem. I also encourage them to keep in contact with me by e-mail after they graduate. I've found e-mail to be particularly useful for communicating with former students who don't reside in the United States.

REASONS WHY STUDENTS MAY WANT TO COMMUNICATE WITH A TEACHER OUTSIDE OF CLASS

There are a number of reasons why a student may seek help from and/ or want to meet with a teacher outside of class. A number of them are dealt with in this section. The order in they're discussed isn't intended to be significant in any way.

Course-Related Tutoring

A student may need a little help to understand or to do some of what's been dealt with in class. There, of course, is a limit to the amount of tutoring that is reasonable for a student to expect from a teacher. You may want to encourage students whose tutoring needs exceed what you're able to provide to either seek help from peers or drop the course and possibly retake it after they've acquired the necessary information and skills to understand and/or do what's required.

Information or Skill Enhancement

A student may be interested in going beyond what's been presented in class and wants your advice for doing so. Such advice could include references to books, journal articles, and websites, and/or information about workshops and other learning experiences. Or a student may be interested in arguing about or discussing with you a position you've taken in class. Time spent with a student doing either of these is likely to be time well spent.

Information Sharing

Students may want to meet (or otherwise communicate) with you because they have information in which they believe you'll be interested. It could be from articles, books, or websites or from personal experience. While much of the information that students shared with me over the years I already had, some was information I didn't have that contributed significantly to my teaching and research.

Issues Concerning Performance on Examinations

Performing poorly on an examination or anticipating doing so are among the more common reasons why students arrange to meet with an instructor.

With regard to performing poorly, students are likely to attempt to do one or more the following:

- Offer a believable excuse for not doing well so that they will continue to be considered a good student by their instructor.
- Raise their grade by arguing that they shouldn't have lost points (or as many points) for some of the answers for which they lost them.
- Get an extra-credit assignment.

And with regard to anticipating performing poorly, students are likely to be seeking advice for either preparing for a specific examination or for coping with test anxiety that may be sufficiently severe to impair their performance on many (perhaps most) of the examinations they take. Helping them cope with a generalized test anxiety is likely to require a referral to a psychologist, perhaps one affiliated with your institution's counseling center.

Academic and Vocational Counseling

You'll certainly be expected to provide these kinds of counseling for your advisees. They're also likely to be requested by students who aren't your advisees, particularly ones interested in your field or your specialty within it. You'd be wise, incidentally, to check with a student's advisor before giving him or her more than superficial academic counseling. While most are unlikely to object to your being helpful to their advisees in this way, some will become angry if you do so without their permission, which could affect adversely the enthusiasm with which they'll support your bid for tenure.

Encouragement

All of us occasionally have bad days and need encouragement to keep motivated. When students have doubts about their abilities academically, they may want to talk about their concerns with a teacher whom they trust and respect. You should, of course, avoid offering encouragement when it isn't warranted. However, when this is the case, you should try to counsel in a way that's unlikely to demolish a student's self-concept.

Getting to Know and Be Known by the Instructor

Some students are highly motivated to get to know their instructors as people, particularly if they consider them role models and/or regard them as being famous. Some students also want some of their instructors to get to know them as people. One reason could be to maximize the likelihood that they'll be both able and motivated to write strong recommendation letters to accompany their applications for jobs, admission to graduate school, or financial aid.

Transference and Counter-Transference

Both of these concepts, which are from Freudian psychoanalysis, are applicable to the teacher-student relationship. With transference in this context, the student develops feelings of "love" for the teacher. This almost always happens when a teacher becomes a role model or mentor for a student. And with counter-transference in this context, the teacher develops feelings of "love" for the student.

A little transference can facilitate learning because it causes the student to be motivated to please the teacher—that is, to do well in his or her course. It can also cause the student to want to spend time with the teacher (e.g., during his or her office hours). When it gets beyond a low level, it can cause problems and possibly even result in unwarranted charges of sexual harassment. To reduce the likelihood of having to cope with such charges (which, fortunately, I've never had to), I almost always keep the door of my office open while meeting with students.

Counter-transference is highly unlikely to have any educational value and acting out on it (particularly with undergraduate students) could conceivably result in charges of sexual harassment, immediate termination, or denial of tenure. While it isn't particularly unusual for younger faculty and older graduate students to fall in love, such relationships can cause problems, even if the student is no longer a student of the teacher.

Reporting Cheating and Plagiarism by Other Students

Occasionally, a student may want to meet with you to report cheating or plagiarism by another student. While I'd be willing to meet with a student for this reason, I'd exercise considerable caution with regard to acting on the information that he or she provided. Charges of cheating and plagiarism are very serious, and I wouldn't accuse a student of either without evidence that was extremely compelling. I'd rather make the error of allowing a student to get away with cheating or plagiarism than of falsely accusing a student of either. I would, however, observe a student who had been so accused closely in the future for evidence of these.

Help for Coping with Conflicts with Other Faculty Members

I usually don't encourage students to meet with me for this reason, particularly if the faculty member is in my department. However, sometimes a student who arranged to see me for another reason will seek this kind of help. If the advice I'd regard as appropriate would be for the student to meet with the faculty member and communicate his or her concerns, I'd probably give it. If, however, the faculty member was acting in a way that appeared to be completely inappropriate and harmful to the student, I'd probably informally report it to my chairperson or dean. And if he or she had received similar complaints previously, some action will hopefully be taken.

Seeking Advice Concerning Personal Problems

Some faculty are both interested and competent to do such counseling and others are not. If a student seeks such counseling from you and you don't want to do it, I believe that you do have an obligation (possibly even a legal one) to both make an appropriate referral and encourage the student to follow through on it. You would certainly have this obligation (at least morally) if a student seemed to be very depressed and/or suicidal.

STRATEGIES FOR MAXIMIZING THE LIKELIHOOD OF BEING PERCEIVED BY STUDENTS AS AVAILABLE AND HELPFUL OUTSIDE OF CLASS

A number of strategies have been suggested (directly or indirectly) elsewhere in this chapter for maximizing the likelihood of being perceived by students as available and helpful outside of class. Some of the more important of these are dealt with in this section. The order in which they're dealt with isn't intended to be significant.

Be Flexible in Your Availability to Students

Be willing to meet with students at times other than your office hours if there's a legitimate reason for their being unable to meet with you when they're scheduled. Also, make yourself available to students through e-mail, voice mail, campus mail, snail mail, and fax.

Give Students Your Full Attention—Really Listen to What They Have to Say

Be available to students in mind as well as body. When you meet with them, really listen to what they have to say. Give them your full attention. By not doing so you're likely to infuriate them as much—perhaps even more—than you would if you weren't available to meet with them. And their anger could cause them to give you lower teaching ratings than they would otherwise.

Whenever Possible, Inform Students About Options Rather than Giving Them Advice

When students seek advice about a problem, the thing you can do that's likely to be the most helpful to them is to increase their awareness of the possible options for solving it and the benefits and losses that could result from implementing each. By doing so, you're likely to empower them to cope with the problem better than they would have been able to otherwise. You'll also be providing a model for selecting a course of action that they can use in the future.

Avoid Making Recommendations That Are Likely to Be Impractical

A student is unlikely to consider a recommendation helpful that it would be almost impossible for him or her to implement. Consequently, in addition to considering the possible benefits and losses from implementing each option for coping with a problem, the practicality of doing each should also be considered.

Challenging Students to Achieve More than They Thought They Were Capable of Achieving

Perhaps one of the most valuable ways that teachers can be helpful to students outside of the classroom is by challenging them to achieve more than they thought they were capable of achieving. This can be done by encouraging them to test certainties (beliefs) about their limitations that they've either never tested or haven't tested recently. They'll probably experience some success if they do so.

Make Referrals Whenever They Seem Warranted

While nobody expects you to be able, by yourself, to help students solve all of their problems, you do have an obligation to be as helpful as you can to them. One way that you can be helpful to them is to make appropriate referrals whenever doing so seems warranted.

Do What You Can to Avoid Becoming a Defendant in Sexual Harassment and Other Student-Related Litigation

You're more likely to do things that could result in your becoming a defendant in student-related litigation when you're interacting with them on a one-on-one basis outside of a classroom than when you're interacting with them in a classroom. It's crucial, therefore, to be aware of the kinds of behaviors that can be considered sexual harassment and avoid doing them. It's also crucial to be aware of other behaviors that can get you into legal difficulty with students and their families (e.g., giving a student a low grade without adequate justification).

Find Reasons to Enjoy Being Helpful to Students Academically

One way to conceptualize the role of a teacher at the college level is being helpful to students academically. While teaching may not be the aspect of working in academia you enjoy the most nor may the time you spend with students outside of class be an important determiner of your success in academia, you're likely to be spending a lot of time with them. Consequently, if you're willing to accept my conception of your role as a teacher, you can make the time you spend with students more pleasant by finding reasons to enjoy being helpful to them academically. A number of possible ones are indicated in this chapter and elsewhere in the book.

15

Creating the Impression of Being Warm with a Good Sense of Humor

Students are likely to rate those teachers whom they regard as being warm with a good sense of humor a little higher than others. While this undoubtedly is due, in part, to the fact they like them, it's also likely to reflect the fact that they learn more from them. They tend to pay more attention to (i.e., are less bored by) and/or are more anxious to please such teachers.

Comments by some of the students whom we interviewed provide a little insight into how teachers behave whom they tend to perceive as being warm with a good sense of humor. I'll be sharing some of these comments with you here. Before doing so, however, we'll look at the potential benefits and losses from a teacher being perceived by his or her students as warm with a good sense of humor.

POTENTIAL BENEFITS AND LOSSES FROM A TEACHER BEING PERCEIVED BY HIS OR HER STUDENTS AS WARM WITH A GOOD SENSE OF HUMOR

My primary focus throughout this book has been on maximizing student ratings. The surest way for a teacher to achieve this goal is to be helpful to students. Consequently, it's necessary to consider the following question before going further: Do students tend to gain more than they lose from a teacher whom they regard as being warm with a good sense of humor?

Students would tend to lose more than they would gain from such a teacher if it resulted in their either not paying as much attention to or being less anxious to please him or her. I know of no compelling evidence to support this conclusion. On the other hand, there is considerable compelling evidence in the education literature that supports the opposite conclusion. Your own experience as a student is also likely to do so. It would appear reasonable to conclude, therefore, that students considering an instructor to be warm with a good sense of humor is highly unlikely to either reduce their attention to or desire to please him or her.

Another possibility for more being lost than gained by students viewing an instructor as warm with a good sense of humor would be it resulting in their respect for him or her being less than otherwise. Again, there's no compelling evidence for this outcome being likely and substantial research and anecdotal evidence for the opposite being true.

It would appear, therefore, that students are unlikely to be harmed by viewing their instructors as warm with a good sense of humor. They are, in fact, likely to learn more than they would otherwise by doing so. And since instructors who are viewed in this way tend to get higher ratings from students, their being so is likely to yield a win-win situation.

SOME DO'S FOR BEING PERCEIVED AS WARM WITH A GOOD SENSE OF HUMOR IN A TEACHER-STUDENT RELATIONSHIP

These do's were abstracted from comments by students about the characteristics of teachers whom they perceive as being warm with a good sense of humor. The order in which they're discussed doesn't necessarily reflect how often they were mentioned.

Learn Students' Names

Students are likely to assume that a teacher doesn't really care about them as people if he or she doesn't learn their names. They're particularly likely to do so if the class is relatively small or they've has a course previously from him or her. Students, of course, are unlikely to regard any teacher as being warm whom they believe only values them as classroom seat-occupiers.

If you're a person (like me) for whom it's extraordinarily difficult to learn names, you may want to communicate this to your students along with the message that you really do care about them as people. While your doing so will not eliminate the possibility that they'll hold it against you when they do their ratings, it does tend to make it at least a little less likely.

Get to Know Students as People

There are a number of ways that you may be able to get to know at least some of your students as people (assuming, of course, they're interested in your doing so). One would be to inquire about their plans for the future. Another would be to discuss the possibility of writing recommendations for them for graduate school or a job. And still another would be to really listen to them and try to be helpful when they seek your help.

Be Approachable

The less you distance yourself from students (i.e., the less you conduct yourself as an all-knowing professor rather than a person), the more likely they are to consider you warm and approachable. Furthermore, they're more likely to do so if you don't, verbally and/or nonverbally, discourage their attempts to approach you that are appropriate.

Be Available to Students

Students are likely to regard being warm and being available as synonymous. Some strategies for influencing students' perceptions of a teacher's availability are presented in Chapter 14.

Show Students That You Respect Them

Students are unlikely to regard a teacher as warm whom they doubt respects them. You can demonstrate respect for students by not talking down to them or otherwise treating them like children or people who are cognitively impaired.

Talk *to* Rather than *at* Students

Students are unlikely to regard a teacher as being warm whom they believe doesn't really attempt to communicate with them. A teacher who talks *to* rather than *at* students will, for example, maintain eye contact with them and modify what he or she says based on how they reacted to what he or she said. Such a teacher will be in rapport with his or her students rather than with himself or herself. Lecturing for him or her will not be primarily a self-stimulation activity.

Use Appropriate Humor When It Is Appropriate to Use Humor

Many of the students whom we interviewed mentioned that an instructor having a good sense of humor tended to make bearable listening to material in which they previously had little interest (usually that which was a part of their liberal arts core, such as philosophy or theology). They also mentioned that an instructor having a good sense of humor helps them to keep their attention focused on material in which they do have some interest, particularly in classes that last for several hours.

Humor to which students are likely to react positively is that which is both appropriate to what is being discussed and not a put-down to someone (i.e., mean-spirited). They are also likely to react positively to humor that suggests the instructor doesn't take himself or herself completely seriously (e.g., humorous anecdotes about his or her errors or shortcomings).

Interact Occasionally with Students as a Person Rather than as a "Professor"

Doing so tends to facilitate their viewing you as warm (i.e., human). I've shared with students, for example, my love for rummage and garage sales, my looking forward to shopping in supermarkets on weekends to get free food samples, and my experiences as a barker at an amusement park.

Admit When You're Unsure of an Answer or Position or When You've Been Wrong About One

Admitting when you're unsure or have been wrong conveys the message to students that you're aware and accept being fallible (i.e., not a God). This increases the likelihood that your students will regard you as being both warm and approachable.

Admitting you've been wrong can also convey another message to your students, perhaps the most important one that you'll ever be able to convey to them. This message (which is a component of the scientific method) is that all answers, positions, and conclusions should be regarded as *tentative* and subject to change whenever new information makes it necessary to modify them. Consequently, if your students want to behave in a manner that's consistent with the scientific method, they'll have to be willing to respect the right of others to be wrong occasionally. And they'll have a right to expect others to respect their right to do so also.

16

Encouraging Students to Be Curious

The items that were dealt with in previous chapters appear on almost all teaching rating forms. While encouraging students to be curious doesn't appear on most such forms, comments by several of our interviewees suggest that students really appreciate instructors who attempt to do so, and it tends to cause them to rate such instructors at least a little higher than they would otherwise (a "halo" effect). Consequently, encouraging students to be curious is an appropriate topic for this book not only because it enhances their potential to contribute to society, but also because it's likely to be a way to increase your teaching ratings.

CURIOSITY AND EXPLORATION

Curiosity and exploration are linked in the psychological literature (Keller, Schneider, & Henderson, 1994; Voss & Keller, 1983). Curiosity is the stimulus, motivation, need, or drive and exploration is the result. While there is universal agreement that curiosity and exploration exist, there appears to be considerable disagreement about the mechanisms responsible for them. Some authorities tend to view the mechanisms as primarily physiological (i.e., instinctual) and others as primarily psychological (i.e., learned). Some support for the former comes from experiments on animals (including mice and rats) that appear to indicate their presence. And some support for the latter comes from observations (e.g., on young girls) that suggest not rewarding curiosity and exploratory behavior causes them to occur less often.

The curiosity-exploration sequence can be triggered by a state of uncertainty that produces psychological discomfort. It's unlikely to be triggered merely by not knowing. While I may not know why a phenomenon occurs, I may not be aware of a reason why it's important for me to know and, consequently, not knowing would be unlikely to produce enough psychological discomfort to motivate me to try to explain it. On the other hand, not knowing the reason for a phenomenon that I observed in my research is likely to produce an adequate amount of psychological discomfort to motivate me to try to do so.

The curiosity-exploration sequence may not be triggered when there is a state of uncertainty that produces psychological discomfort if an even greater state of psychological discomfort is anticipated by it being triggered. Negative attitudes of others toward an exploration can result in such an anticipation. Adolescent boys during the last century, for example, were discouraged from masturbating by being told by their parents that doing so would cause them to go insane.

Curiosity, like fire, can have both positive and negative consequences. On the negative side, it can cause experimentation with illegal drugs. However, like fire, the benefits from encouraging its use are likely to far outweigh the losses. High curiosity has been shown, for example, to be a major motivator for great accomplishments.

There appears to be almost universal agreement among authorities on curiosity and exploration that the frequency at which the curiosity-exploration sequence is triggered can be influenced (at least a little) by a number of psychological and sociological factors, including the following:

- Societal mores and taboos.
- The attitudes of the person's significant others, including family, friends, and the authorities in his or her profession.
- The attitudes of the person's teachers.
- The person's awareness of uncertainty and/or its relevance.

The impacts of some of these are dealt with elsewhere in the chapter.

CURIOSITY AND CREATIVITY/INNOVATION

Curiosity facilitates creativity and innovation. And creativity and innovation are essential if our students are to contribute to their community and/or society to the extent to which they're capable. Consequently, a goal of teaching should be to enhance our students' inclination to be curious whenever we have the opportunity to do so.

DISCOURAGEMENT OF CURIOSITY IN ACADEMIA

While there isn't universal agreement about a teacher's ability to enhance a student's "genetic" propensity for curiosity, there is such agreement about a teacher's ability to thwart it. The attitudes that teachers communicate while lecturing and otherwise interacting with students can affect the likelihood of both their students' curiosity being aroused and such arousal resulting in exploration.

There are a number of ways that a teacher can, subtly or not so subtly, thwart his or her students' curiosity and/or motivation to explore, including the following:

- Presenting information as facts, rather than as theories, hypotheses, constructs, or judgments.
- Encouraging students to view as facts the opinions of authorities.
- Discouraging students from questioning the status quo for theories, constructs, and what the establishment considers to be facts.
- Encouraging students to believe that it's possible for questions to be answered definitively.
- Overly stressing the need for adequate scientific justification for satisfying curiosity by exploring.
- Focusing on learning answers rather than on asking questions.
- Allowing your biases (i.e., theoretical points of view) to discourage research that could invalidate them.
- Failing to encourage students to evaluate information appropriately.

Each is discussed below.

Presenting Information as Facts, Rather than as Theories, Hypotheses, Constructs, or Judgments

Viewing something as being a fact suggests that there isn't any need to explore it further. Doing so, therefore, is likely to discourage curiosity and exploration. One of the rules of the scientific method is that all conclusions (i.e., facts) should be regarded as tentative and subject to change whenever new relevant information becomes available. Consequently, it is desirable to present information as theories, hypotheses, constructs, or judgments that it may or may not be worthwhile to explore further. Some "facts," of course, have been verified so often that doing so again is unlikely to be time well spent.

Encouraging Students to View as Facts the Opinions of Authorities

The opinions of authorities, even highly respected ones, can be wrong. At one time, for example, almost all authorities believed that the earth was flat and that the other planets in our solar system revolved around it rather than the sun. Students should be encouraged to view the opinions of authorities as simply opinions (rather than as facts) because doing so is less likely than otherwise to dampen their curiosity about and/or dissipate their motivation for exploring them. They should be made aware, however, that questioning such opinions can lead to their being ridiculed and/or otherwise would cost them. Even Albert Einstein (one of the handful of persons who most influenced twentieth-century thought) experienced such consequences for questioning the adequacy of Newtonian physics.

Discouraging Students from Questioning the Status Quo for Theories, Constructs, and What the Establishment Considers to Be Facts

Persons who are a part of the establishment in their field are likely to discourage students (directly or indirectly, verbally or nonverbally) from questioning the status quo for theories, constructs, and what are considered to be facts because they have an ego-investment in them. Change is anxiety arousing as is the possibility of having to change. Discouraging exploration that could result in a need to change is an almost instinctive thing to do (and I've done it). Perhaps discouraging students less often from exploring for this reason is a more realistic goal than never doing so.

Encouraging Students to Believe That It's Possible for Questions to Be Answered Definitively

As I've indicated previously, adhering to the scientific method requires that all answers be regarded as tentative and subject to change whenever new relevant information becomes available. Some answers, of course, have been confirmed so often that new information is highly unlikely to be unearthed that would make it necessary to change them. While students who want to explore such questions further shouldn't be discouraged from doing so on the basis that they've already been answered, they should be made cognizant of the fact that doing so is less likely to yield data that will necessitate changing an answer than would be exploring questions for which the accuracy of answers is less certain.

Overly Stressing the Need for Adequate Scientific Justification for Satisfying Curiosity by Exploring

Establishing scientific justification for an exploration requires answering the "So what?" and "Who cares?" questions. While being able to provide cogent answers for these questions increases the likelihood of a paper being accepted for publication in a scholarly journal, it should not be viewed as an absolute requirement for satisfying curiosity by exploring. Basic science does not have such a requirement (although some funding agencies for basic research may have). And tacit knowing (Polanyi, 1967) can arouse curiosity and motivate worthwhile exploration before it's possible to answers these questions cogently.

Focusing on Learning Answers Rather than on Asking Questions

The primary focus in much college teaching is on having students learn answers to questions rather than on asking questions, including ones pertaining to the accuracy of the answers they're expected to learn. While it's certainly justifiable to acquaint students with the existing state of knowledge in a particular field (or segment thereof), they should also be encouraged to ask questions that will enable them to assess its accuracy. That is, while they should be told that "Columbus sailed the ocean blue in 1492," they should also be encouraged to ask how we know that he did. I believe strongly that one of our primary goals as teachers should be to enhance our students' ability to evaluate information. This goal is discussed elsewhere in the chapter.

Allowing Your Biases (i.e., Theoretical Points of View) to Discourage Research That Could Invalidate Them

Many scholars are likely to interpret an attack on a theoretical point of view to which they adhere strongly similarly to how they would interpret one on themselves or their children. Consequently, they're likely to discourage students from pursuing research that could either cast doubt on the validity of their point of view or support an alternative one. Graduate students who are shrewd will attempt to identify their thesis or dissertation committee members' biases before seeking their approval for a topic.

It's extremely difficult to keep your ego and theoretical biases from impacting on your students' choices of topics for research. It may seem that you're placing your reputation as a scholar at risk by not doing so because their data may fail to support your theoretical points of view. Actually, the opposite is likely to be true. Two of the persons in my field who were most highly respected as scholars were ones who were strong advocates for theoretical positions that where shown to be invalid. Shortly after this happened, each acknowledged being wrong "in print" and adopted a theoretical position that was consistent with the available data. In both cases, their reputations as scholars were enhanced by their willingness to acknowledge having been wrong when the data necessitated their doing so.

Failing to Encourage Students to Evaluate Information Appropriately

As I've indicated previously, I believe that one of our main objectives as teachers should be to facilitate our students' learning how to evaluate information. One way that we can do this is to encourage them to attempt to answer the following three questions whenever they're attempting to determine the amount of confidence that they can have in the validity and reliability of research-based data or other information:

• What do the words with which it is being communicated mean?
• How does its promulgator know?
• What then?

Each is discussed below.

The first step in evaluating information is understanding what it means—that is, what is being communicated. What some of the words mean to you may not be what they're intended to mean. It's necessary, of course, to understand a message before you can assess its accuracy or utilize the information in it.

The next step is assessing the likelihood of the information being accurate. You need to know at least a little about the source of the data (observations) on which conclusions are based. The amount of confidence that you can have in the accuracy of information can be specified on a continuum and your task is to make judgments about where specific information (data) falls on it.

The final step in this evaluation process is utilizing the information (assuming, of course, that you have confidence in its accuracy). You would attempt to identify some of the theoretical and/or practical implications it may have. Doing this could, of course, arouse your curiosity and lead to exploration.

STRATEGIES FOR AROUSING STUDENTS' CURIOSITY

There are a number of ways by which you may be able to arouse your students' curiosity sufficiently to motivate them to explore, including the following:

• Talk about questions that haven't been answered adequately and the reasons why it's important for them to be. You may also want to talk about methodologies by which they could be answered more completely and/or accurately.

• Reinforce your students' curiosity, even when the exploration it is likely to motivate probably won't be fruitful. Of course, if you can nudge their curiosity toward a path that's likely to yield worthwhile information, so much the better.

- Mention whenever it's appropriate to do so the rule of the scientific method which states that all answers should be regarded as tentative and subject to change whenever new information becomes available.

- Point out questions that need to be answered whenever it's appropriate to do so and suggest some theoretical and/or practical implications that each of the possible answers to a question could have.

- With students who seem to respect you and view you as a role model, talk enthusiastically about the pleasure you derived from specific explorations (research) that resulted from your curiosity being aroused.

- Provide some assignments (perhaps for extra credit) that will give students experience formulating answerable questions and/or evaluating information (see Chapter 18 for suggestions).

17

Textbook Selection Issues

Regardless of whether the teaching rating form your students use contains an item pertaining to the textbook selection, their feelings about the texts and other materials you require them to purchase are almost certain to affect how they feel about you as a teacher and, consequently, the ratings they'll give you. If they really like you, they'll tend to rate you a little higher on almost all of the items on the form. And if they really dislike you, they'll tend to do the opposite. Consequently, one way to maximize your teaching ratings is to be cognizant of students' likes and dislikes when selecting the textbooks and other materials (e.g., CD-ROM multimedia software) you'll be utilizing.

Students' likes and dislikes are, of course, not the only relevant considerations when selecting textbooks and other materials for teaching them. Content and organization are also. They are among the most important (if not the most important) considerations for textbook selection.

We'll be focusing here on a number of issues you'd be wise to consider when selecting textbooks and other materials that students are required to purchase. The order in which they're discussed isn't intended to be significant. The ones pertaining to students' likes and dislikes were derived from comments made by undergraduate and graduate students in a structured interview survey that dealt with the features of textbooks that they did and did not find helpful (see Appendix D in Silverman, 1998).

THE APPROPRIATENESS OF HAVING STUDENTS PURCHASE A TEXTBOOK OR OTHER MATERIAL FOR A COURSE

Textbooks and other materials that students are required to purchase are tools. They only have value if they significantly facilitate their learning. If they cost students more than the value they provide for meeting course objectives, then the appropriateness of requiring that they be purchased will be questionable.

Every semester I receive order forms from our bookstore on which to specify the required texts and other materials for the courses I'll be teaching the next semester. One message that this routinely conveys to faculty is that there should be at least one required text for every course. Certainly, it is appropriate to require students to purchase textbooks (or other materials) if they are likely to significantly facilitate their learning. However, to merely require students to purchase textbooks to use as a reference or for a chapter or two may not only be questionable from the educational point of view, but it's also likely to anger them, particularly if the textbooks or other materials are expensive. And their anger is likely to result in your receiving lower teaching ratings than you would have otherwise. Consequently, it would be better for your presumption to be no required text for a course rather than one or more.

There are, of course, alternatives to having students purchase course materials. They can be placed "on reserve" at your library. This option tends to be more practical for relatively small enrollment courses than for relatively large enrollment ones. They can also be placed on a website if all of your students are able to access the Internet. The number of students in a class obviously isn't a consideration if course materials are made available to students in this way. Internet distribution of such materials is dealt with elsewhere in this chapter.

CUSTOM VERSUS GENERIC TEXTBOOKS

Your textbooks can either be ordered from a publisher or be created by you. If you opt for the latter option, you'll either have to write a textbook or edit a "coursepack." The latter is an anthology that consists largely (or wholly) of journal articles and book chapters that were selected and organized to reinforce and/or enable students to explore in greater depth what the instructor presents in class. A coursepack may also contain material that was authored by the instructor specifically for it.

Written permission to reproduce a journal article or book chapter in a coursepack must be obtained from the copyright holder. For a journal article, the holder is likely to be the journal in which it was published rather than its author(s). A fee may be charged for reproducing such an article or book chapter.

Your college bookstore probably will be willing to handle the printing, binding, and distribution of coursepacks. It may even be willing to secure the necessary permissions from copyright holders and pay permission fees. The bookstore would recover what it paid for permission fees when the coursepacks were sold to students.

Coursepacks are usually designed and intended to be used in a specific course at a specific institution. However, a coursepack may be assembled that would be likely to be adopted at other institutions if it were available to them. This would most likely be a coursepack for a course in an emerging area or for one that is taught in a non-traditional way. There are firms (with websites) that would handle the permission-securing process for and the printing, binding, and distribution of such a coursepack. An alternative would be to self-publish it (see Silverman, 2000, for the practical information needed to do this both economically and efficiently).

If there is at least one textbook available for each of your courses that has the appropriate content and organization and is written at the appropriate level with the appropriate theoretical orientation, it probably wouldn't be worthwhile for you to create custom textbooks. However, if an appropriate one is not available, it may be worthwhile for you to create one for your course and for similar ones at other institutions. I did this for all six of the courses I teach. (The books were published by the Prentice Hall and Allyn & Bacon divisions of Simon & Schuster.) If you decide to consider this option, you're likely to find the information in Silverman (1998) helpful.

My primary objective in this book is to help you develop a record during your probationary period that is at least adequate for meeting your department's minimum requirements for tenure. Unfortunately, creating appropriate texts for your courses may not be helpful for developing such a record. It may, in fact, do the opposite. The publication and grant-securing requirements for tenure are among the most important in many departments and colleges. If your publication and grant-seeking records are considered marginal by the tenured faculty in your department and they're aware that you've spent a great deal of time creating materials for your courses, they may attribute your doing so to a lack of ability or interest in being a scholar and, as a result, not support your bid for tenure enthusiastically. For information needed to cope successfully with the publication requirements for tenure, see Silverman (1999).

INTERNET PUBLICATION AND DISTRIBUTION OF TEXTBOOKS AND OTHER COURSE MATERIALS

The Internet was just beginning to impact significantly on the publication and distribution of textbooks and other course-related materials when this chapter was written. Two of the ways it was doing so are described in this section.

Textbooks have been published on websites. For a fee (payable by credit card) students can read them on a monitor, or download and print them, or purchase a printed copy. The site on which they could be accessed is owned either by a firm that specializes in publishing books in this way or by the book's author(s). If the website is owned by such a firm, the author is almost always paid a royalty for each copy that is sold.

Chapter files are usually updated either periodically or continually. Consequently, a textbook that is published in this way has the potential to both start out and remain more up to date than it would if it were printed. The delay between the completion of the manuscript for a printed textbook and its publication is likely to be a year or more.

The Internet is also being used for distributing textbooks. There are Internet bookstores that sell both new and used copies at a discount. Textbooks purchased from such sites are also cheaper than ones purchased from college bookstores for another reason—no sales tax.

THE APPROPRIATENESS OF THE CONTENT FOR THE COURSE

Judging the appropriateness of the content of a textbook for a course requires that it be evaluated from at least four perspectives:

- The relevant information that's presented.
- The information presented that isn't relevant.
- The relevant information that isn't presented.
- The biases and theoretical points of view of the author(s).

Some implications of each of these for selecting an appropriate textbook are indicated in this section.

The Relevant Information That's Presented

This is perhaps the most important of these considerations. The higher the percentage of the topic covered in a course that are dealt with in a textbook, the more appropriate it would tend to be as a required text for that course.

The Information Presented That Isn't Relevant

There are likely to be at least a few topics in any textbook that aren't dealt with in a course for which it's adopted (except perhaps one taught by its author). The higher the percentage of the topic covered in a textbook that are dealt with in a course, the more appropriate it would tend to be as a required text for that course.

Students are likely to become angry if a relatively high percentage of the information in a textbook they're required to purchase isn't relevant for the course that they're taking. They're particularly likely to be angry if the book won't be used as a text for that material in other courses they'll be taking. Such anger could result in their rating how a course was taught a little lower than they would otherwise.

The Relevant Information That Isn't Presented

When evaluating the appropriateness of a book's content for a course, it's necessary to determine the number of topics not covered in it that are dealt with in the course. The higher the percentage of the topic dealt with in a course that aren't dealt with in a textbook, the less appropriate it would tend to be as a required text for that course.

Students tend to resent having to purchase several textbooks for a course, particularly if they regard them as being expensive. Consequently, adopting a textbook for a course that fails to deal with so many of the topics that are dealt with in it that it's necessary to require a second textbook should be avoided if at all possible. An alternative, of course, when there isn't a textbook with appropriate content is to produce either a custom one or a coursepack.

The Biases and Theoretical Points of View of the Author(s)

All authors have biases and their biases influence their theoretical points of view and, consequently, the content of their books. They determine what topics will be dealt with and how much space will be devoted to each. They also determine how each topic will be presented. A theory, for example, is likely to be presented differently by an author who has an ego investment in it than by one who doesn't.

You'd be wise to adopt textbooks whose authors share most of your theoretical points of view. If you frequently criticize the points of view presented in a textbook that you required students to purchase, they're likely to wonder why you required them to do so. And if the book is expensive, they may become angry with you for requiring them to buy it. Such anger could, of course, adversely affect the teaching ratings that they give you.

THE APPROPRIATENESS OF THE ORIENTATION FOR THE STUDENTS

The orientations of textbooks that are intended for a particular course can vary considerably in a number of ways, including the following:

- The degree to which they stress research (scientific) issues.
- The degree to which they stress humanistic (e.g., ethical) issues.
- The degree to which they stress practical issues.
- The degree to which they focus on "forests" rather than "trees."

Some of implications of these for textbook selection will be considered here.

The Degree to Which They Stress Research (Scientific) Issues

Some textbooks intended for a particular course cite considerably more research than do others. A text that deals with research in considerable depth is likely to be more appropriate for courses in which most of the students are majors than for ones in which most are non-majors.

The Degree to Which They Stress Humanistic (e.g, Ethical) Issues

Texts for courses for students who intend to become healthcare or education practitioners are likely to be more humanistic in their orientation than those for similar courses for ones who intend to become researchers. An example of such a course would be an introductory statistics and research design one.

The Degree to Which They Stress Practical Issues

Texts for courses for students who intend to become healthcare or education practitioners are likely to be more practical in their orientation than those for similar courses for others. Such courses could include psychology ones.

The Degree to Which They Focus on "Forests" Rather than "Trees"

An old, but true, adage suggests that it's relative easy "to lose the forest for the trees." Some texts intended for a particular course focus on details (i.e., "trees") more than do others. Those that do so tend to be more appropriate for courses for majors than for non-majors.

THE APPROPRIATENESS OF THE ORGANIZATION FOR THE COURSE

The more closely the sequencing of topics in a textbook conforms to that in a course, the more appropriate it is for use in it. This consideration isn't, however, as crucial as that for content for at least two reasons. First, it's frequently possible to modify the order that topics are presented in a course to conform to that in a textbook. And second, when this isn't possible, reading assignments can be made from the text's index rather than its table of contents.

THE NUMBER OF HOURS THAT IT'S LIKELY TO TAKE STUDENTS TO READ AND/OR OTHERWISE UTILIZE THE MATERIAL

The amount of time that it would take students to read and/or otherwise utilize the relevant material in each of the texts that could be adopted for a course may be an important consideration in the selection of a text for it. If that for a particular text is likely to exceed what it would be reasonable to expect students to spend, it probably wouldn't be a good idea to adopt it because doing so could anger them and result in your receiving lower teaching ratings than otherwise.

THE AMOUNT THAT STUDENTS HAVE TO PAY FOR THEM

The more expensive the textbook(s) and other materials that students are required to purchase for a course, the more likely they are to become angry at the instructor and rate his or her teaching a little lower than they would otherwise. If students are only required to purchase a single textbook, anger from this source is probably less likely to adversely affect teaching ratings than that from some of the others that have been mentioned. However, if they're required to purchase more than one text and together they cost more than they're used to spending for the texts for a course, their anger could be sufficient to significantly reduce the ratings that they give the instructor. Consequently, if you are requiring students to purchase multiple texts for a course, you'd be wise to both acknowledge the total cost being high and provide cogent reasons for all of them being necessary. You might even want to place one or more on reserve, thereby providing students with an option to purchasing them.

IF THE AUTHOR IS ALSO THE TEACHER

Using a book that you authored as a text can yield both benefits and losses. If the book was based on the course, the main benefit is likely to be its content, organization, and orientation being completely (or almost completely) appropriate for the course. A second possible benefit would be enhancing your credibility with students as being someone who is knowledgeable about the content of the course. And a third possible benefit could, of course, be extra income.

There unfortunately are also several ways you could lose by using a text that you authored. One would be students perceiving your lectures as being very similar in content to your text and concluding that the time they're spending in class isn't being well utilized. A second would be their assuming that the main reason you're using your own text is to make money from them. And a third would be their assuming that they're being exposed to only one of the viable points of view on important theoretical and practical issues. The latter could be a legitimate concern if the various points of view on important issues weren't presented evenhandedly.

As I've indicated previously, I use texts I've authored for all the courses I teach. My primary reason for using them is their appropriateness for the content, organization, and orientation of the courses. A secondary reason is that I can require students to get at least some of the material from them on their own and, thereby giving me more time to spend in class on other things. While I've probably paid a price for doing this (with regard to ratings), I believe that it's far outweighed by the benefits my students have received from my doing it (even though they're often not consciously aware of them until after they graduate).

THE AVAILABILITY OF WEBSITES AND OTHER ANCILLARIES

Some textbook publishers give ancillaries to instructors who adopt their texts, particularly ones for large enrollment undergraduate courses. Such ancillaries could include testbanks, multimedia CD-ROMs, videotapes, audiotapes, overhead transparencies, slides, ideas for teaching particular concepts or units, and/or websites. All of these are likely to make it less time-consuming for an instructor to teach a course well (but in, of course, a generic way). Be aware, however, that books for which there are ancillaries tend to be more expensive than ones for which their aren't any because the cost of producing them is almost always considered when setting a price for the book.

THE USER-FRIENDLINESS OF THE MATERIAL

Some textbooks, because of the way they're designed and/or written, tend to be more user-friendly for students than are others. We've done extensive interviewing with students about the features of textbooks that they do and don't find helpful. Some of what we learned is summarized here.

Features That Tend to Make Textbooks User-Friendly

Features that the students we interviewed mentioned as increasing the helpfulness of textbooks included the following:

- Lots of headings and subheadings.
- At least one margin on a page that's wide enough for writing comments.
- For each chapter, an outline of what's going to be covered at the beginning and a summary at the end.
- Suggested readings for exploring at least the most significant topics in greater depth.
- Photographs and drawings are both supportive to the text to which they're intended to be relevant and located close to it.
- Flowcharts and other figures summarize things talked about in the text.
- Definitions are highlighted (e.g., boldfaced, italicized, or printed in a different color).
- There are personal experiences or stories about how the information being presented applies to everyday life.
- Examples are meaningful to students and possibly even humorous.
- Photographs are in color rather than black and white.
- Sentences are relatively short and concise.
- Main points are repeated.
- At least some of it is written in the first (rather than third) person.
- Paragraphs are relatively short and make a single point.
- When matters are controversial, the author describes the various points of view and indicates which he or she finds most compelling and why.
- There are a lot of short chapters rather than a few relatively long ones.
- The table of contents includes the main chapter subheadings.
- Information about the author that can facilitate making the interaction between student and author more personal.
- The paper on which it is printed can be written on with a pencil.
- Pictures have captions and the captions clearly indicate what students are to attend to in them.
- There are study questions in the chapters that don't just ask for facts but can facilitate students gaining awareness of some implications of the information.
- Answers to calculation exercises are printed in the book.
- The author attempts to communicate rather than just rattle off facts.

Features That Tend to Make Textbooks User-Unfriendly

Features that the students we interviewed mentioned as reducing the helpfulness of textbooks included the following:

- References being given in numbered footnotes that are at the ends of chapters or the back of the book.
- Page after page of text that isn't broken up in some way—e.g., by headings, subheadings, or illustrations.

- Photographs and drawings—including cartoons—that don't really help to make what's being discussed in the text more meaningful.
- Being talked down to by the author (i.e., being treated like a young child or someone who is cognitively impaired).
- Photographs and/or references not being recent when there's no obvious justification for it.
- One research study or case study after another being cited.
- Frequent statements that something alluded to will be described in a later chapter.
- Pages with narrow margins and small type.
- Many long lists of references in parenthesis at the ends of sentences.
- Going from one topic to another without any real transition.
- More than three levels of subheadings.
- Written on too high a level to be easily read.
- Assuming knowledge that students perhaps should, but don't, possess.

18

Encouraging and Facilitating Student Research

This chapter differs somewhat from previous ones in that it doesn't deal with an item that appears on most teaching rating forms. Yet it can affect how a junior faculty member is perceived as a teacher. Those who encourage and direct student research tend to be perceived by chairpersons, deans, members of promotion and tenure committees and others who make tenure decisions as being more dedicated to teaching than those who don't. At a recent promotion and tenure committee meeting in which I participated, for example, most of the members considered the dedication of a candidate to teaching doubtful until it was pointed out that she was the only one in her department who both encouraged students to do and directed masters theses. A number of issues will be dealt with in this chapter that are relevant to encouraging and/or facilitating student research.

WHY ENCOURAGE STUDENTS TO DO RESEARCH?

There are a number of reasons why encouraging and facilitating student research may enable you to meet your responsibilities to your students and department more successfully and enhance your rewards from teaching. Some of the more important of these are considered in this section. The order in which they're dealt with isn't intended to be significant.

Formulating Answerable Questions, Answering Them, and Testing Hypotheses Are Basic Abilities That a College Education Should Facilitate Developing and/or Enhancing

While few of your undergraduate students will probably be scholars and do publishable research, all of them will be required almost every day to formulate answerable questions, answer them in ways that are likely to yield correct answers, and/or test hypotheses. If they're to be successful in meeting these obligations, they'll have to be familiar with and know how to utilize the scientific method. One way that they can both increase their familiarity with the scientific method and hone the skills they need to utilize it in both their professional and their personal life is to do a research project. Consequently, doing research can help them acquire at least a few of the basic skills that a college education is supposed to help them acquire.

Formulating and Answering Answerable Questions and Testing Hypotheses Are Abilities That Employers Expect Their Employees Who Are College Graduates to Have

Problem solving and decision making on the job require these skills. They facilitate acquiring and evaluating information. The more opportunities we give our students to practice doing them, the better able they'll probably be to do them for their employer. One way to help our students develop these skills is to create opportunities for them to do research.

Encouraging Students to Do Research Can Enhance Your Reputation as a Scholar

Few faculty develop strong national reputations as scholars that don't have students involved with their research. Developing such a reputation usually requires a fairly large number of publications and most faculty who are unable to devote at least half of their time to research can't generate them on their own. One way that faculty who have a full teaching load may be able to publish sufficient research to develop such a reputation is by having students gather at least some of their data.

A question can legitimately be raised about the appropriateness of involving students with your research if your purpose for doing it is just to develop a national reputation. If, however, your main reason for pursuing a program of research was to contribute to an existing body of knowledge, then the appropriateness of involving students with it in this way would be far less questionable.

Another question that can legitimately be raised about the appropriateness of involving students with your research concerns the amount they're likely to learn when what they're researching wasn't their idea and may even be a topic in which they have little interest. A case can be made for their involvement having the potential to be a good learning experience for them even if both are true. Many of the skills that they need to hone to become competent as researchers aren't content specific. They're essentially the same for research in physics, psychology, and history. The methodologies used for making observations and analyzing data are different, but the same scientific-method-based rules apply. Consequently, students are likely to benefit, at least a little, by participating in such research.

Encouraging Students to Do Research Can Help You Satisfy the Publication Requirements for Tenure

There are at least two reasons why involving students with your research can facilitate your complying with the publication requirements for promotion and tenure. First, doing so can enable you to publish more articles than you'd probably be able to otherwise. And second, members of promotion and tenure committees tend to respond positively to publications that resulted from the person they're considering collaborating with students, as long as he or she is the first author of at least some of them.

Involving Students with Your Research Can Increase Your Impact on Your Field

The more data you can gather and publish, the more impact you're likely to have on your field. Consequently, having students help with data gathering has the potential to increase the amount of it you'll be able to gather and, thereby, your probable impact on your field.

Encouraging Students to Do Research Can Both Demonstrate and Document Your Dedication to Teaching

Teaching can take place in the "laboratory" as well as in the classroom. Your potential for impacting on students may, in fact, be greater in the former than in the latter because you'll probably be teaching them one-on-one. Consequently, you can both demonstrate and document having a genuine interest in teaching by being proactive in encouraging students to do research with you. Letters from students whom you've taught in this way can be included in the dossier that will be used to support your bid for promotion and tenure (see Chapter 19).

Directing Student Research Can Be Both Enjoyable and Rewarding

One of the main reasons why I've been proactive in encouraging students to collaborate with me on research during my 30-plus years in academia is that I've both benefited from and thoroughly enjoyed such collaborations. I've benefited from them in at least two ways: They've helped me to remain "mentally alive" and their questions about and challenges to some of my positions (while dialoguing with me about their research) have forced me to rethink them.

THE STUDENT–RESEARCH DIRECTOR RELATIONSHIP

The amount of time and energy you're likely to have to invest in directing a student's research will be determined, at least in part, by his or her ability to function independently. Consequently, a student–research director relationship, like an employer–employee one, can be conceptualized metaphorically as being one of the following:

- a master–servant relationship.
- a principal–agent relationship.
- an employer–independent contractor relationship.

Some possible implications of it being each of these will be considered here.

A Master–Servant Relationship

In a master–servant relationship, the master tells the servant what to do and the servant does it. This is the usual type of relationship between a research assistant and the faculty member to whom he or she was assigned. A student functioning in this role would be unlikely to contribute significantly to deciding what to research and how to do it. However, he or she would almost always be informed about why it was decided to research a particular thing and to use a particular methodology for doing it. The student's contributions would be likely to be acknowledged in any publications in which data were presented that he or she contributed significantly to gathering and/or analyzing, but the student wouldn't be listed as an author or co-author on any of them. Listing him or her as one would, in fact, be considered unethical by almost all scholars.

A Principal–Agent Relationship

A student who is in a principal–agent relationship contributes to defining the problem to be researched and/or the methodology for doing it. This is the most dependent type of relationship that's likely to be considered acceptable for a thesis or dissertation (i.e., a master–servant relationship would be highly unlikely to be considered acceptable for either). The research director closely supervises the project and usually has "the last word" when there are disagreements. The student would be a co-author of any publications resulting from the research. Whether the student or the research director would be listed as first author would be determined by the contribution of each to defining the problem, designing the study, collecting and analyzing data, and preparing the manuscript. The student would be more likely to be listed as second than as first author.

An Employer–Independent Contractor Relationship

The research director in an employer–independent contractor relationship would function mainly as a consultant. The student would assume the primary responsibility for defining the project, designing procedures for data acquisition and analysis, collecting and analyzing data, and drafting the manuscript(s). This mode of functioning would certainly be desirable for doctoral dissertations. Because the student is assuming the primary responsibility for the project, he or she would be the first author or possibly even the sole author. If the research director contributed very little to the project because the student was able to function independently, the research director would probably be acknowledged rather than listed as a co-author.

COPING WITH STUDENTS' RESISTANCE TO DOING RESEARCH

Many students who aren't majoring in a science are likely to doubt their ability to do research and, consequently, they're likely to resist trying to do it. Furthermore, they're likely to assume that research isn't something they'll enjoy doing, thereby further reducing their motivation for doing it. You're going to have to modify these attitudes if you're to be maximally successful in getting students to do research.

Perhaps the best way to convince students that they don't lack the ability to do research and can derive pleasure from doing it is to have them do a small research project that they're likely to be able to complete successfully and enjoy doing. This can be done by making such a project a course requirement. I did this in my clinical research methodology course for more than 10 years. All of our graduate students who were training to be clinicians had to take this course. Very few of them prior to taking it had either done research or viewed themselves as being capable of doing it. A requirement for the course was to either replicate a study that was published in one of our journals or do a small study in an area of interest. Both the topic and methodology had to be approved by me. I discouraged students from doing studies that they'd be unlikely to either be able to complete or enjoy doing. The data from more than 25 of these studies have been published. And many of the students after completing their project acknowledged being at least a little less certain that they lacked the ability to do or could enjoy doing research.

RESEARCH OPTIONS FOR STUDENTS

There are a number options for giving students a research experience. They vary with regard to the nature of the experience and the role that is played by the research director (i.e., the type of collaboration). Some implications of both are dealt with here.

Types of Collaboration

There are a number of responsibilities that you could have in the research you do with students. What they are in a particular instance will be determined, at least in part, by the nature of the collaboration. Several of the more common types of collaboration between research directors and students are described here.

Research Assistant

In this type of collaboration, the research director usually tells the student both what to do and how to do it. The student assumes little or no responsibility for either defining the problem or selecting (or developing) methodologies for data collection and analysis. Two ways that students are likely to benefit from having such an experience are gaining a deeper understanding of the research process and learning how to do at least a few research-related tasks.

Second Author

In this type of collaboration the student assumes some responsibility for defining the problem and/or selecting (or developing) methodologies for data collection and analysis. He or she is also likely to be at least partially responsible for data collection and analysis and for drafting parts of the article in which the data are reported. The research director, however, assumes the primary responsibility for defining the problem, selecting or developing methodology, and preparing the article for publication. If more than one faculty member was actively involved with the research, the student may be listed on the article as third or fourth author.

First Author

The student in this type of collaboration assumes primary responsibility for defining the problem and selecting (or developing) methodologies for data collection and analysis. Furthermore, the student is responsible for the collection and analysis of data and he or she has the primary responsibility for drafting the document in which the data are reported. This is how a student is supposed to collaborate with the chairperson of his or her thesis or dissertation committee.

Types of Projects

There are a number of ways that you may be able to get students involved with research. Some of them are indicated here. The order in which they're dealt with isn't intended to be significant.

Gathering and/or Analyzing Data for You

If you have a grant for your research program, you may be able to employ a few students to assist with data gathering and/or analysis. Even if you can't pay students, there may still be some who'd be interested in volunteering to assist you in order to be able to document having had such experience. Undergraduate students who can document having had this experience are probably more likely than otherwise to be offered a research assistantship by at least one of the graduate colleges to which they apply.

Class-Related Projects

There are at least two ways that class projects can serve as a vehicle for providing students with research experience. The first is requiring each student in the class to independently define and do a small research project. An example of how I've used this approach is presented elsewhere in the chapter.

A second option would be having all of the students in the class participate in a group project. The topic would be selected by the instructor. The students as a group would develop the methodology (protocol) for making observations. Each student would gather a little data using the agreed-upon methodology. The data would then be combined and each student would receive a copy and be told to both analyze it in the manner that he or she considered most appropriate and draft an article reporting it. If the data possess adequate levels of validity and reliability, the instructor may be able to utilize it. I have several publications in peer-reviewed journals from which some of the data came from this source. I, of course, acknowledged the assistance of the students in gathering it.

Independent Study Projects

At many colleges and universities (including mine), both undergraduate and graduate students can do independent study projects for credit. I've had a number of students who wanted to get some research experience (and possibly also a publication) register for one or two semester hours of credit to do a research project.

I've encouraged graduate students to do research projects as independent study ones rather than as master's theses for two reasons. The first is that their graduation is less likely to be delayed. And the second is that the project can be written up in a format that's appropriate for the journal to which it's intended to be submitted. This format is likely to be different than that for a thesis. A publication in a professional or scholarly journal (particularly a peer-reviewed one) is likely to be more beneficial to both the student and society than a master's thesis of which few people are aware. Furthermore, a study reported in article (particularly if it's published in a peer-reviewed journal) is likely to be more beneficial to the person who directed it than one reported in a thesis because he or she will probably have contributed enough to be listed as a co-author.

Theses and Dissertations

Doing a thesis or dissertation is one of the main ways that students in many fields have traditionally received a research apprenticeship. They, of course, are likely to benefit more from such an apprenticeship if it isn't their first research experience.

STRATEGIES FOR ENCOURAGING STUDENTS TO DO RESEARCH

There are a number of ways that students can be motivated to at least consider the possibility of doing research. Some of them are dealt with here. The order that they're discussed isn't intended to be significant.

Encourage Students to View Themselves as Persons Who Are Capable of Doing Publishable Research

Many students who aren't majoring in a science have great difficulty viewing themselves as being capable of doing publishable research. At least some of the attributes they ascribe to persons who have this capability are ones they believe they don't possess. That is, their stereotypes for such a person don't square with how they view themselves.

There are two ways that you may be able to get students who have such an attitude to question its validity. One is to increase their awareness of the humanness of some of the persons who are widely respected as scientists or scholars in their field or have been in others historically. Make students aware that at least some of them aren't (weren't) any smarter, creative, or dedicated than they are. Relevant passages from their biographies, auto-biographies, or other writings can help to communicate this.

A second way that you may be able to get students who have the attitude to question its validity is by challenging them to test their certainty that they lack some of the abilities needed to do publishable research. One way you can do this is to have them replicate a study that appeared in a recent issue of a journal that publishes letters-to-the-editor and submit a report of their results (either positive or negative) in a letter to the editor of that journal. If the replication was well done and the manuscript is relatively short and well written, it's likely to be published.

Involve Students in Your Program of Research

As I've indicated previously, involving students in your program of research as either paid or volunteer research assistants can both interest them in doing research and help them develop an objective attitude toward their ability to do it. It can also interest them in doing research (e.g., theses or dissertations) under your direction.

"Publish" a List of Possible Research Topics

One of the most respected scholars in my field during the mid-twentieth century (Dr. Wendell Johnson) when he was an assistant professor identified a disorder to research (i.e., stuttering) and defined more than 25 master's theses and doctoral dissertations that he felt would provide the data he needed to comprehensively describe its symptomatology and phenomenology. He posted a list on a wall near his office and was able in this way to attract graduate students to do almost all of them. Such a list now could be posted on a website rather than a wall.

Suggest Possible Research Topics to Students in Class

Point out research needs in your lectures. And then, at least occasionally after doing so, describe briefly the methodology you'd use to do the research and state that if anybody is interested in exploring the possibility of doing it, they should see you.

Reinforce and "Shape" Students' Ideas for Research Projects

When students share research ideas with you that aren't particularly good, don't discourage them. Rather, try to shape them (i.e., indicate in a "face-saving" way how they can be modified to make them both worth doing and doable).

Develop a Reputation as Being Someone Whose Students Complete Their Research in a Reasonable Amount of Time

Graduate students learn through the grapevine whose students tend to complete theses and dissertations in a reasonable amount of time and whose don't. And, everything else being equal, they'll tend to gravitate toward faculty whose students do so to direct their research and avoid those whose don't.

FACILITATING STUDENT RESEARCH

Several issues are dealt with in this section that are relevant for facilitating (directing) student research. They can significantly affect how students evaluate a research experience and, consequently, what they're likely to communicate about it to peers and other faculty (e.g., your chairperson or members of your college's promotion and tenure committee).

The Director's Responsibilities

Your legal responsibilities when directing master's theses and doctoral dissertations are likely to be specified in your institution's faculty handbook. Your other responsibilities when directing student research will depend, in large part, on whether you consider its primary purpose to be learning or demonstrating competence.

If you consider its primary purpose to be learning (as I do), then you will assist students in any reasonable way you can that will either contribute to enhancing their learning experience or to making it more pleasant. Your primary goal will be to teach a process and its related skills, rather than to evaluate their level of understanding of the process and degree of competency using the skills. Evaluating these will also be a goal, but a secondary one. Another secondary goal will be to make the experience sufficiently pleasant that it is unlikely to turn students off to doing further research.

If, on the other hand, you regard its primary purpose as being to demonstrate having the knowledge and competence needed to function independently, then you will restrict the amount of help you give. This conception of the purpose of student research is probably more widely accepted for doctoral dissertations than for other types. There is, however, a significant risk when adhering to it for directing doctoral dissertations. If a student hasn't had considerable research experience prior to doing a dissertation, the process of doing one with minimal direction may be sufficiently unpleasant to discourage him or her from wanting to become a productive scholar (thereby, causing him or her to procrastinate—perhaps too long—on meeting the publication requirements for tenure).

The Student's Responsibilities

Students must assume the primary responsibility for doing the tasks necessary to complete their project in a timely manner, as independently as they can. You'd be unwise to agree to direct the research of any student who isn't willing (i.e., highly motivated) to do this. Having students agree to do it in writing can provide you with a legal "escape clause" when they grossly fail to live up to their obligations and you decide to terminate your research relationship with them.

Students must also assume the primary responsibility for motivating their research director to make their project a priority. Most faculty have many responsibilities—both within and outside of academia. A student's research project is unlikely to become a priority unless he or she does things to make it so. They include exhibiting genuine enthusiasm for the project and gratitude for the assistance provided by the director, gathering data in a way that yields adequate levels of validity and reliability, meeting the research director's deadlines, and gently (like a good secretary) motivating the research director to meet his or her responsibilities for the project. In this regard, it's important to remember that "the squeaky wheel gets oiled." You may want to share this paragraph, or a paraphrase of it, with students whose research you direct.

Publication-Related Ethical Issues

These concern how the contributions of a student to a publication should be communicated in it. They can be communicated by an acknowledgment, or by listing the student as first or sole author, or by listing him or her as a second or third co-author. Criteria for selecting the most appropriate for a particular publication are presented elsewhere in this chapter. It's considered to be a breach of scholarly ethics to be either overly or insufficiently generous when doing so.

19

Documenting Teaching for Promotion and Tenure

> A semantic reaction is the psycho-logical reaction of a given individual to words and language and other symbols and events in connection with their meanings.
>
> —Korzybski, 1958, p. 24

You, of course, want the persons who evaluate your application for tenure to react favorably to the teaching section—that is, have a positive semantic reaction to it. Their reaction to your teaching record will be determined by the meaning—both intellectual and emotional—that it has for them. We will explore some strategies in this chapter by which you may be able to increase the likelihood that their semantic reaction to your teaching record will be a positive one.

THE RESPONSIBILITIES OF THE CANDIDATE FOR PREPARING THE APPLICATION

Your application for promotion and tenure will probably be assembled by your chairperson or one of the other senior faculty members in your department. This person is unlikely to be familiar with all of your relevant activities and accomplishments. It's your responsibility to make him or her aware of them.

There are two basic ways that you can provide the person who is preparing your application for tenure with information about your teaching (and other activities). The first is to give him or her lists and copies of relevant documents (i.e., raw data). The second is to draft the paragraphs in which these data are reported. If you can write about yourself both objectively and well, the latter would probably be your better option. It could also be the better option for the person who is preparing the application because drafting such material tends to be time-consuming.

DOCUMENTING TEACHING FOR PROMOTION AND TENURE

There are a number of ways to document the quality of teaching in a promotion and tenure application. Many of them are dealt with here. The order in which they're considered doesn't necessarily indicate their value for this purpose.

A Statement Giving Your Philosophy of Teaching

Such a statement may or may not be required at your institution (it is at mine). It should come across as sincere and be consistent with your documentation for quality of teaching. If, for example, you indicate in the statement that teaching well both is and has been a priority for you but your teaching ratings and some of the comments that students make in their letters suggest strongly that it hasn't, some members of your committee may question your integrity and/or your ability to objectively evaluate your teaching.

If at some point during your probationary period your teaching ratings were relatively low, you may want to offer an explanation. It would be particularly worthwhile to provide such an explanation if it's one to which the members of the committee are likely to respond positively (e.g., a divorce or the death of a spouse or child).

Your Teaching Load Each Semester (or Quarter) During Your Probationary Period

You should, at a minimum, list the identification numbers and names of the courses you taught each semester and how many students there were in each. You should also list for each semester any other teaching-related responsibilities you had, such as supervising student practicum, directing student research, preparing a new course (or causes), or supervising teaching assistants.

It would be particularly important to detail your teaching load if it had been extraordinarily large throughout most or all of your probationary period and your publication and extramural funding records could be considered marginal. This could cause the members of your committee to be more forgiving than otherwise.

The Student Ratings Each Semester for Each Course You Taught

You'll probably be required to report the student ratings each semester. If you followed the recommendations given in this book for maximizing your teaching ratings, they should be at least minimally adequate to support your bid for tenure.

Continuing Education Courses and Workshops You Taught During Your Probationary Period (at Both Your Institution and Elsewhere) and a Summary of any Evaluations by Participants

Your having received and accepted invitations to teach continuing education courses and workshops is likely to communicate a positive message about both your interest in teaching and ability to teach, particularly if at least some of them were from other institutions. If evaluation sheets were distributed to participants in any of them, you may want to have some of their more positive comments about your teaching quoted in the application.

Theses, Dissertations, and Other Student Research Projects Directed Along with References to Publications and Convention/Conference Papers in Which Their Findings Were Reported

Directing student research is teaching. Consequently, it's appropriate to list the student research projects you've directed as well as any publications and convention/conference presentations they've yielded. You may want to list those of which you are a co-author in the publication section of the application.

A List and Brief Description of Other Teaching-Related Activities with Students

You should document any teaching-related activities in addition to classroom teaching and directing student research with which you've been involved. It's particularly important that this be done well if these activities were very time-consuming and your publication and/or extramural funding records could be considered weak.

Evaluations of Your Teaching by Faculty Who Have Attended Classes or Workshops You Taught

If your department conducts peer evaluations of junior faculty teaching, the reports of those who did them will probably be included in the application. If such evaluations aren't done in your department but some of the faculty from it had sat in on your classes or workshops and been complementary about your teaching, you might want to ask them to repeat their comments in a letter that could be quoted from or included in the application.

Letters from Ex-students Evaluating Your Teaching

Letters from ex-students evaluating your teaching are almost always required. Departments differ with regard to how students are selected to write such letters. In some, they are selected by the department (either randomly or otherwise). In others, they are selected by the candidate. And in still others, some are selected by both.

You'd be wise to find out at the beginning of your probationary period how your department selects students to write such letters. If you'll be selecting at least some of them, begin compiling a list at the beginning of your probationary period of students who appear to respect you highly as a teacher. Also save any greeting cards, letters, and e-mail messages you receive from students that contain positive comments about your teaching.

Letters from students are judged not only by their content, but also by the percentage of those asked to write who do so. A relatively low percentage could be interpreted as indicating that at least some choose not to write because their comments wouldn't be helpful. Consequently, you may want to ask the students whose names you're planning to submit whether they would be willing to write if asked before you submit them.

Teaching Awards You've Received

Both list and describe any teaching awards you've received from your department, college, university, and/or professional association(s). You may want to include a statement about the competition, particularly if the award was a highly competitive one.

Textbooks or Other Teaching-Related Materials You've Authored

You should both list and describe any textbooks or other teaching-related materials you've authored, particularly ones for courses you've taught that have been adopted by instructors of similar courses at other institutions. The fact that a portion of a course you've developed is being taught elsewhere says something positive about your ability to teach.

Your Course Syllabi

Some institutions require course syllabi to be included in applications for tenure. A syllabus can undoubtedly influence committee members' impressions about the quality of a course. See Chapter 4 for suggestions for constructing syllabi to maximize the likelihood of their being reacted to positively.

Performance of Your Students on Examinations Administered by Others

If students who have been enrolled in your courses take examinations administered by others that include material which was covered in them and you can document how well they did on that material, you may want to include the documentation in your application. Such examinations would include licensing, certification, and master's and doctoral comprehensive ones.

Tape Recordings of Classes or Workshops You've Taught

These aren't a mandatory component of the application package for tenure at most institutions. Few tenure committee members would be willing voluntarily to take the time to listen to and/or view them. They can be useful, however, in an appeal for a tenure denial in which a department claimed falsely that the candidate's teaching had been extremely poor. They might do this, for example, if they felt that the candidate wasn't a team player (i.e., they perceived the candidate as being deficient with regard to collegiality). Such a deficiency can be extremely difficult to document. Consequently, a department may claim that a deficiency in teaching and/or publication is the reason for their not supporting a candidate.

Evaluations of Your Teaching Record by External Reviewers

Most institutions don't routinely do this for teaching records (though they do for research ones). They can be requested by a department to strengthen its case for denying tenure because of inadequate teaching. And they can be requested for a tenure-denial appeal by either the candidate or the department to support his, her, or its case.

FACTORS THAT CAN AFFECT THE SEMANTIC REACTION TO THE TEACHING SECTION OF A TENURE APPLICATION

There are a number of factors that can affect the semantic reaction to the teaching section of a tenure application. Some of them are indicated in this section.

The Amount of "Meat" in the Documentation

The greater the amount of evidence presented to support a teaching record that's likely to be perceived by tenure committee members as being credible, the greater the likelihood that they'll consider the record to be adequate.

Student Ratings of Teaching

In spite of the fact that faculty tend to question the validity and reliability of such ratings, they're likely to be given considerable weight when judging teaching adequacy for tenure, particularly if they've consistently been either exceptionally low or exceptionally high. Exceptionally low ratings throughout the probationary period are likely to be interpreted as indicating either a lack of ability to teach well or a lack of interest in doing so. And exceptionally high ratings throughout this period could be interpreted as indicating either teaching excellence or overly striving to be liked by students. The comments that the students who are asked to evaluate the candidate's teaching make in their letters will probably indicate which it is.

Consistently low teaching ratings can be particularly detrimental for persons who try for tenure before their "up or out" year. Some committee members may feel that denying them tenure can motivate them to improve their teaching. About the only scenario I can think of when low teaching ratings are likely to be ignored is when a candidate has a huge grant and is threatening to leave if not tenured immediately.

The Amount of Padding in the Documentation

Members of tenure committees tend to be turned off by material they consider padding. An example of such material is course handouts. An excessive amount of teaching-related padding tends to be characteristic of applications in which the candidate is trying to compensate for (or mask) a relatively weak publication and/or extramural funding record.

The Percentage of Students Who Were Invited to Write Letters and Wrote Them

The higher this percentage, the more likely the quality of a candidate's teaching is to be perceived as being at least adequate (assuming, of course, that almost all of the comments about his or her teaching were positive).

The Amount of Enthusiasm Evinced by Letter-Writers

The more enthusiastic the letter-writers are about a candidate's teaching, the more weight their letters are likely to be given for supporting the case for granting tenure. This is true for letters from students as well as those from faculty who attended sessions of the candidate's courses or workshops.

Negative Comments by Letter-Writers and Other Evaluators

Even a single negative comment about a candidate's teaching can hurt his or her tenure case, particularly if it isn't the candidate's "up or out" year and his or her publication and/or extramural funding is relatively weak.

Whether the Candidate Is Seeking Promotion and Tenure Before His or Her "Up or Out" Year

As I've indicated previously, a stronger teaching record is likely to be needed to be tenured before the "up or out" year than at it.

How Well the Material Is Organized and Written

Members of promotion and tenure committees tend to respond more positively to applications that are very well organized and written. A relatively poorly written and organized application (i.e., one on which little time appears to have been spent) may be interpreted as indicating that the department isn't particularly interested in tenuring the candidate now.

The Availability of Faculty to Teach His or Her Courses

If a candidate who is being considered in the "up or out year" is marginal as a teacher and it would be extremely difficult to find a replacement to teach his or her courses, the candidate is more likely to be tenured than he or she would be otherwise. A department is particularly likely to argue that tenure should be granted for this reason if the candidate has an excellent publication and/or extramural funding record.

The Excellence of the Candidate's Publication and Extramural Funding Records

While these shouldn't affect judgments of teaching adequacy, they often do, particularly in cases where the quality of a candidate's teaching is marginal rather than poor. The presence of an excellent publication and/or extramural funding record can either increase or reduce the likelihood that a department will enthusiastically support a candidate for tenure. While it will in most cases increase the likelihood of such support, it can reduce it if there are senior faculty in the department who have relatively weak publication or extramural funding records (the reason being professional envy or jealousy). Furthermore, such faculty may feel that the presence of a productive scholar in their department could make them look bad, particularly to upper administration.

The best protection that a junior faculty member can have against this source of bias is upper-administrative support (dean level or higher). While a relatively weak department may not be thrilled about having a productive scholar on its faculty, upper administration is likely to be so because they can add his or her accomplishments to their "brag" list.

The Value That the Institution Places on Teaching Well

While all colleges and universities want their faculty to teach well, some give teaching more weight when making tenure decisions than do others. Research universities, for example, tend to give teaching less weight than do liberal arts colleges.

The Institution's Attitude Toward Appeals and Litigation

Denial of tenure can lead to appeals and litigation. These can be time consuming, expensive to defend against, and damaging to the reputation of the institution (particularly if the person denied tenure is a woman or member of a recognized minority). Consequently, an institution may be reluctant to deny tenure on the basis of inadequate teaching unless it is able to document the candidate's teaching being so extremely well.

The Candidate's Reputation with Regard to Collegiality

The informal interviewing I've done of senior faculty at a number of institutions suggests that a lack of collegiality was the real reason for some persons being denied tenure when the reason given was inadequate teaching and/or publication. A deficiency in collegiality is usually more difficult to document than one in teaching or publication. A denial of tenure on this basis is probably more likely to lead to appeals and litigation than one on the basis of teaching or publication. Persons who are unwilling to be team players don't tend to be tolerated any better in academia than they are in business.

A FINAL COMMENT

If you keep the teaching section of your promotion and tenure application in mind right from the beginning of your probationary period, you're likely to be better able to adequately document your teaching record than if you begin thinking about it near the end. You may, in fact, want to begin a file in which you collect such things as unsolicited letters from students that comment positively on your teaching and the names of students who'd be likely to be willing to write such letters.

20

Teaching Beyond Tenure

> Tenure has been said to give a free ride to the lazy and those whose careers have languished. . . . A number of legislatures around the country have supported a "post-tenure review" process, in which tenured individuals would be evaluated.
>
> —from a position paper on the Faculty
> Page of the Auburn University website

My primary focus throughout this book has been on teaching for tenure. Certainly, a college or university faculty member is expected to continue teaching well after receiving tenure and becoming an associate professor. He or she can be penalized in several ways for not doing so. Annual salary increases for associate professors at many colleges and universities are based on merit, which includes teaching. And a requirement for promotion from associate to full professor at most colleges and universities is continuing to teach well.

Until recently, once a person was tenured, he or she almost always had it for life. Post-tenure review bills had been passed or were being considered by the legislatures in a number of states when this chapter was written. A post-tenure review could cause an associate or full professor to lose tenure (and possibly be fired) if he or she ceased teaching adequately or being productive as a scholar. Post-tenure review initiatives and their possible consequences are explored in this chapter along with some issues, challenges, and opportunities for teaching beyond tenure.

POST-TENURE REVIEW

Some persons cease doing the preparation necessary to teach well after receiving tenure and others do so after being promoted to full professor. They also may cease being productive as scholars. Traditionally, what a college or university could do to rid itself of tenured faculty who have ceased being productive has been limited to denying them merit salary increases, taking away their graduate standing, and/or if they are associate professors, refusing to promote them to full professors. Recent articles in the *Chronicle of Higher Education* suggest that this situation may be changing in at least a few states and could change in others if post-tenure, review-based tenure revocation survives legal challenges. Undoubtedly, at least some academics who lose tenure on this basis will sue for its reinstatement. They may well be able to argue cogently that post-tenure review functions like an ex post facto law and, consequently, is not applicable to faculty who have been tenured for a number of years. This argument, of course, is unlikely to be usable by faculty who are currently untenured. Consequently, teaching well is something that presently untenured and future faculty will probably have to do throughout their academic careers.

When this chapter was written, post-tenure reviews usually resulted in a warning if teaching adequacy was found to be lacking. The threat of loss of tenure was usually sufficient to motivate those receiving such a warning to improve their teaching sufficiently to raise their student teaching ratings and other indices of teaching quality to an acceptable level.

POST-TENURE TEACHING ISSUES AND CHALLENGES

Several teaching-related issues and challenges are considered here that are particularly relevant for tenured faculty.

Having Teaching Continue to Be a Career Rather than a Job

A career that ends up consisting of sets of routines becomes a job. If you teach the same courses every semester or every year for a number of years, you are likely to develop a set of routines that will enable you to teach them with very little thought. This is particularly likely to happen if increasing demands are made on your time by administrative, committee, professional association, scholarly, extramural-funding-seeking, and/or family responsibilities. Teaching in this way (on automatic) is unlikely to be particularly pleasurable for you nor particularly helpful for your students. The transformation of teaching from a career to a job is likely to be a very gradual process, one of which you may not become aware until the transformation is almost complete.

It's almost impossible to prevent this from happening in courses that you've taught for a number of years. It is possible, however, to limit it. One way to do this is to change textbooks every few years. Doing so is likely to motivate you to rethink your course's content and organization (to make it consistent with the textbook). And, consequently, you'd be less likely than otherwise to teach it completely "on automatic," at least the first few times you did so.

Motivating Yourself to Continue Investing in Undergraduate Teaching

There are at least two reasons why you may find it difficult to motivate yourself to continue investing in undergraduate teaching (both of which were mentioned in the previous section). The first is an increasing number of demands being made on your time to do tasks that aren't related (at least directly) to such teaching. The rewards you receive from doing them may be greater than those you could get from teaching undergraduates well.

Another reason why you may find it more difficult to motivate yourself to invest in undergraduate teaching is that you don't enjoy doing it as much as you did previously. After you've taught a course a number of times, your teaching of it may become automatic. Consequently, your enthusiasm when teaching it would be likely to be less than it was previously. As a result, the students would be likely to give you lower teaching ratings than they did previously. This would tend to make you feel less appreciated, which could affect negatively both your attitude in class and the amount you invest in preparation. The result could be the formation of a vicious circle with student dissatisfaction leading to reduced investment in teaching, leading to increased student dissatisfaction, and so on. This is particularly likely to happen in departments that reward pursuing scholarly activities (e.g., publication and grant-writing) more than they do teaching undergraduates well.

One way that you may be able to keep yourself motivated to invest in undergraduate teaching is to develop and teach undergraduate courses you haven't taught previously. These can be either existing courses or new ones that you develop. It may be possible for you to teach an existing course you haven't taught previously if the faculty member who teaches it leaves. The job description for his or her replacement could include teaching the course (or courses) you no longer want to teach. And there may be an opportunity for you to develop a new course when one is needed to fill a void in the curriculum. Such a void in a healthcare field, for example, is likely to be created whenever the scope of practice for its practitioners broadens to include a new type of responsibility.

Another way that you may be able to keep yourself motivated to invest in teaching well is to view doing so as contributing to your legacy. Most academics would like their impact on their field to endure after they retire or die. This is one of the reasons why they are likely to continue writing articles and books for publication after being tenured. That is, they are likely to believe that their writings will continue impacting on their field long after they cease being active as scholars. While this will be true for a few of them, it won't for most. Few students and scholars read articles and books that are more than 25 years old. And those who do so are likely to read them more for historical interest than for new ideas. Consequently, the legacy that published books and articles provide is likely to be a relatively short-term one.

How, then, can you create a professional legacy that will continue to impact on your field long after your retirement or death? The way that you're most likely to be successful in doing so is through your students. They're likely to perpetuate some of your points of view for at least another generation. And if a few of them become academics, your points of view are likely to continue to resonate in your field for additional generations, long after your books and articles cease being read.

Coping with the Need to Remain Up-to-Date

Most college teachers are tenured at least six years after receiving their terminal degree and they're likely to continue modeling at least some of the courses they teach on comparable ones that they took while in college. Assuming that their teachers were up-to-date, a lot could have happened in the years between then and now to make the points of view they presented either invalid or unfashionable.

The longer you teach, the more likely you are to become out of date in one of these ways, particularly on topics that aren't directly pertinent to your scholarly pursuits—that is, ones on which you haven't gone out of your way to keep up with the literature. You're probably more likely to be so by presenting points of view that are no longer fashionable than you are ones that have been shown to be invalid. An explanation for a phenomenon may go out of fashion for reasons other than it being invalid. Regardless, students expect you to present accurate information that's state-of-the-art for fashion. They're usually willing to hear arguments, however, for why what has ceased being fashionable should be again.

If you teach courses outside of your research interests, particularly if they are fairly broad survey ones, you're unlikely to have the time to keep current on all of the topics covered in them. Perhaps the best you can do is to select textbooks for such courses that have been widely adopted because they're considered both accurate and current with regard to fashion.

Coping with a Snowballing Generation Gap

The longer you teach, the wider the generation gap is likely to become between you and your undergraduate students. Examples that were meaningful to them at the beginning of your teaching career may no longer be so ten or more years later. Their expectations, backgrounds, priorities, and work ethics may also change dramatically. Your failure to cope successfully with such changes is likely to cause you to have a poorer rapport with your students and, as a consequence, receive lower teaching ratings from them.

Perhaps the best way to cope with this gap is to not assume that your students' expectations, backgrounds, priorities, and work ethics are the same as those of your generation nor that those of your students now are the same as they were a few years ago. Your ability to remain competent as a teacher will depend, in large part, on your adeptness at spotting and coping successfully with such changes.

Coping with Burnout

College teachers are no more immune from experiencing burnout than are those in other professions. There are a number of reasons why college teachers can experience burnout. Among those that they may be able to cope with (at least a little) are the following:

- Teaching the same courses in the same way for many years.
- Having poor rapport with students.
- Receiving poorer teaching ratings than previously.

Strategies for coping with them are considered below.

Teaching the Same Courses in the Same Way for Many Years

Doing this can lead to boredom which, in turn, can lead to burnout. To reduce the likelihood of this occurring, you may want to teach your courses a little differently each time and/or swap the ones you teach every five years or so.

Having Poor Rapport with Students

A loss of rapport can result from changes in your students' expectations, backgrounds, priorities, and/or work ethics that you fail to recognize. They are unlikely to either spend more time than absolutely necessary with you or trust you if they don't believe you understand them and their needs. The greater the gap between your generation and that of your students, the more you are going to have to extend yourself if you are to continue having a good rapport with them.

Your rapport with students could also slip if teaching well became less of a priority for you than it was previously. For example, you may have proven to yourself that you can teach well and moved on to meeting other challenges (e.g., grant-writing or establishing a national reputation as a scholar). While your colleagues may welcome your doing this, your undergraduate students are unlikely to do so.

Receiving Poorer Teaching Ratings than Previously

Several tenured professors have indicated to me that they burned out on teaching for this reason and others have made comments to me that suggested they have also. It's difficult to maintain your enthusiasm for doing something when you believe that what you're doing isn't being appreciated. Your best insurance against burning out as a teacher for this reason is continuing doing what you can to maximize your teaching ratings after receiving tenure.

POST-TENURE TEACHING OPPORTUNITIES

There are teaching opportunities you're more likely to have after receiving tenure than prior to doing so. Some of them are mentioned here. The order in which they're dealt with isn't intended to be significant.

Authoring College Textbooks and Other Teaching Materials

Many college teachers, particularly those at research-oriented institutions, delay authoring textbooks and other teaching materials until they've been tenured. In fact, doing so is recommended for faculty at such institutions by the Text and Academic Authors Association (Silverman, 1998).

Authoring college textbooks is like lecturing. It differs from classroom lecturing in several ways. First, the medium used is the printed rather than the spoken word. Second, lectures can be accessed by students at more than one point in space-time. Third, students can easily review parts of a lecture. Fourth, lectures are likely to be relatively free of tangents. And fifth, lectures can be accessed by students at more than one institution.

For practical "how to" information about textbook and other academic book authoring, see Silverman (1998). Topics that are dealt with in it include qualifications necessary for securing a contract from an academic publisher, potential benefits and losses from authoring textbooks and other academic books, preparing a proposal, submission strategies for academic book proposals, negotiating a publishing contract, negotiating a joint collaboration agreement with co-authors, finding the time to write a book-length manuscript while carrying a full faculty load, preparing the manuscript, meeting production- and marketing-related responsibilities, and avoiding an IRS audit.

Teaching Continuing Education Courses and Workshops

As your national (or international) reputation as a scholar or practitioner in your field becomes stronger, the number of invitations you'll receive to teach continuing education courses and workshops outside of your institution is likely to increase. Many tenured faculty (including me) thoroughly enjoy such teaching and also find it rewarding financially. They enjoy doing it because most of those who attend are there because they want to be and participants tend to be very appreciative as long as some of the information presented is relevant to their interests and responsibilities.

Lecturing to Persons Outside of Your Field

As you become better known outside of your field, invitations to do such lecturing are likely to increase. It can be either to persons in fields that are related to yours or to the general public. And it may be done under the auspices of your institution or another.

Visiting Professorships

These are more likely to be available to tenured than to non-tenured faculty. And institutionally, they're more likely to be tolerated for tenured than for non-tenured ones, particularly if they're for longer than a semester. Unfortunately, the receipt of such professorships by junior faculty can trigger professional envy or jealousy that can cause them problems when they go up for tenure.

HOW DO YOU KNOW WHEN IT'S TIME TO RETIRE FROM COLLEGE TEACHING?

While I've used maximizing student teaching ratings as a "carrot" throughout this book, my primary objective has been to provide information that can enable junior faculty and others to make their teaching more effective and also more enjoyable for both themselves and their students. Junior faculty who do well as teachers and scholars are likely to become senior faculty, and when they reach an age at which retirement could be appropriate, they'll have to decide whether it's appropriate for them. I've reached such an age (68), and in order to get some help deciding whether it's time for me to retire from college teaching, I informally surveyed a number of senior faculty (some of whom had already retired) for circumstances that could indicate it may be time to do so. Those mentioned included the following:

- You can afford to retire financially.
- Your physical and/or mental abilities are no longer adequate to continue teaching.
- You are no longer productive as a scholar nor intend to be again.
- Teaching has ceased being fun.

- You can no longer connect well with students.
- You've failed an institutionally mandated post-tenure review of teaching.
- Your chairperson or dean wants you to retire.
- Your spouse wants you to retire.
- You've found an activity (or activities) to engage in that you enjoy doing more.

Deciding how much weight to give each is, of course, highly subjective. You may have to make the decision to retire almost completely on the basis of one of them (e.g., if your physical and/or mental abilities were no longer adequate to continue teaching). For me, an important consideration would be the requirement of my professional association's Code of Ethics "to hold paramount the welfare of persons served professionally." The persons who I am serving professionally as a teacher are my students, and when I cease being able to teach them adequately (regardless of the reason), I would definitely consider that to be an appropriate time to seriously consider retiring from teaching.

References

Anderson, C. W. (1993). *Prescribing the Life of the Mind*. Madison: University of Wisconsin Press.

Cashin, W. E. (1995). *Students Ratings of Teaching: The Research Revisited*. IDEA Paper No. 32. Manhattan: Kansas State University, Center for Faculty Evaluation and Development.

Feigl, H. (1955). The Scientific Outlook: Naturalism and Humanism. In Herbert Feigl and May Brodbeck (Eds.), *Readings in the Philosophy of Science* (pp. 8–18). New York: Appleton-Century-Crofts.

Johnson, W. (1946). *People in Quandries*. New York: Harper & Brothers.

Keller, H., Schneider, K., & Henderson, B. (Eds.) (1994). *Curiosity and Exploration*. Berlin, Germany: Springer-Verlag.

Kimball, B. A. (1988). Historica Clamitatum. In Bruce A. Kimball (Ed.), *Teaching Undergraduates* (pp. 11–22). Buffalo, NY: Prometheus Books.

Korzybski, A. (1958). *Science and Sanity: An Introduction to Non-Aristotelian Systems and General Semantics* (4th ed.). Lakeville, CT: Institute of General Semantics.

Polanyi, M. (1967). *The Tacit Dimension*. Garden City, NY: Anchor Books.

Silverman, F. H. (1995). *Communication for the Speechless* (3rd ed.). Boston: Allyn & Bacon.

Silverman, F. H. (1998). *Authoring Books and Materials for Students, Academics, and Professionals*. Westport, CT: Praeger.

Silverman, F. H. (1999). *Publishing for Tenure and Beyond*. Westport, CT: Praeger.

Silverman, F. H. (2000). *Self-Publishing Books and Materials for Students, Academics, and Professionals*. Greendale, WI: CODI Publications.

Voss, H.-G., & Keller, H. (1983). *Curiosity and Exploration: Theory and Results*. New York: Academic Press.

Woldkowski, R. J. (1978). *Motivation and Teaching: A Practical Guide*. Washington, DC: National Education Association.

Index

About the Author

FRANKLIN H. SILVERMAN is a Professor of Speech Pathology at Marquette University (Milwaukee, Wisconsin) and a Clinical Professor of Rehabilitation Medicine at the Medical College of Wisconsin (Wauwatosa, Wisconsin). He has authored approximately 150 papers in professional journals and a dozen books, including three that deal with academic publishing and tenure: *Authoring Books and Materials for Students, Academics, and Professionals* (Praeger, 1998), *Publishing for Tenure and Beyond* (Praeger, 1999), and *Self-Publishing Books and Materials for Students, Academies, and Professional* (2000). Dr. Silverman is a Fellow of the American Speech-Language-Hearing Association and a Fellow and past president of the Text and Academic Authors Association. He is a recipient of the Marquette University Faculty Award for Teaching Excellence, Emerson College's Alumni Achievement Award, and the Disabled Children's Association of Saudi Arabia Prize for Scientific Research on Rehabilitation. His biography has appeared in *Who's Who in the Midwest, Who's Who in America, Who's Who in the World, Who's Who in Medicine and Healthcare*, and *Who's Who in World Jewry*. Dr. Silverman has served for a number of years on both his department's and college's faculty development and promotion and tenure committees.